John Abulafia is a playwright and director. Most recently, he has written a six-part TV serial commissioned by Channel 4 about the Israeli invasion of Lebanon. He has directed at many theatres, run three companies and has a broad repertoire ranging from Shakespeare to new plays. He is a regular member of the National Theatre's education team, working with children. In the last few years he has begun to direct opera, and has worked at the English National Opera and Glyndebourne as well as staging new operas with a company he founded – Mecklenburgh Opera. His novella, *Foolscap*, is published by Faber.
He lives in London and has two teenage children.

JOHN ABULAFIA

# Men and Divorce

*Coping, Learning, Starting Afresh*

FONTANA/Collins

First published in 1990 by Fontana Paperbacks
8 Grafton Street, London W1X 3LA

Copyright © 1990 by John Abulafia

Printed and bound in Great Britain by
William Collins Sons & Co. Ltd, Glasgow

*For Dorothy Manner and*
*Shona Hyatt Williams*

# Contents

# *Introduction*

You have picked up this book because separation or divorce is somehow an issue in your life at present.

Is this book going to help you? Try this simple test. Here is a couple discussing their ailing marriage:

HIM:    Darling, I think it's time we faced facts.

HER:    I agree, darling. Our marriage isn't working.

HIM:    That's how I feel. It's sad, but I think we should get divorced. What do you think?

HER:    I agree with you.

HIM:    No hard feelings?

HER:    Of course not. I'll always be your friend, you know that.

HIM:    Thanks. I'll move out tomorrow, OK?

HER:    Fine. Don't worry about me.

HIM:    And don't you worry about me.

BOTH:    I'll be fine! (*hugging each other tenderly*) Thanks for everything. Bye!

If your marriage ended, or could end, like this, then don't waste your money; close the book and put it back on the shelf.

But perhaps you read that dialogue and thought, 'This is rubbish. Life isn't like that.' You're right. That dialogue isn't just fictional, it's phoney; in fact, it's crap. When real couples split up, it is messy and people get hurt; and the hurt lasts.

Despite the fact that our society has come to accept that men and women are equal, we have to face the fact that the sexes can differ in the way they respond to an emotional crisis like divorce.

This book is about the way men experience the trauma of divorce. This is a book that both analyses that experience, and then explores ways in which men can come to terms with the hurt, and learn from it.

If you read that dialogue and thought, 'These people aren't real; I know what it's like to split up with some-one . . .' then this book can help you. It's about men, but it's not exclusively for men. I hope men, women and, indeed, couples will read it.

I have based this book on sixty interviews I conducted over a period of eighteen months. These were with divorced men. When using a section of an interview in the text, I have transcribed it from the tape, making no attempt to tidy up the speaker's words into neat sentences; I wanted to recapture their voices, characters and behaviour exactly.

I also interviewed a lot of professional counsellors who work with couples who are in the process of splitting up. Many of these experts expressed important ideas in a direct, succinct way. I've incorporated these comments into the book, too.

*Men and Divorce* was born out of my own experience. I had been married for eleven years when my wife and I split up. We have two children, and so I have direct experience of all the issues discussed in this book.

However, I decided quite early on that I would not use my own experience as material for analysis or discussion. I had two reasons. Firstly, I could offer all my other interviewees and their families anonymity; I could not do this for myself, my ex-wife and children. Secondly, I could not have that vital objectivity about my own experience that you must have if you are to write clearly and helpfully about an emotional crisis. That said, my own experience of divorce proved to be very helpful when it came to understanding what other men were going through.

One final point: this book was written with the intention of helping men help themselves get through the crisis of divorce. That does not mean that the book is full of nice, cosy, comfy hints. I regularly encountered attitudes amongst divorced men that made me so cross I wanted to bang their heads against the wall. I didn't. More often than not I also felt great sympathy for them. However, some of their attitudes seemed very entrenched and were the cause of much unhappiness. There are places in the book where I felt the best way of helping my readers was to attack those attitudes.

So, using a mixture of cool analysis, sympathy and tough talking, I hope *Men and Divorce* will help you through a difficult, challenging phase of your life.

# CHAPTER ONE

# Divorce Is Different for Men

The death of a marriage is a prolonged emotional crisis. When a couple separates and eventually divorces, each partner goes through another, different, upheaval. At the very least, the circumstances of their lives change radically. At worst, they feel the meaning of life is lost and its structure shattered.

There are many books about women and divorce, many more about children and divorce. No one has written a book that aims to help, guide and support the men who are going through this upheaval in life.

This lack of interest in men's experience of divorce is rather revealing. After all, we live in a culture that is still largely dominated by men; the divorce rate has been rising for a long time, and more and more men are going through a period in their lives that is filled with feelings of failure, anger, guilt, loss, remorse, depression, even despair. Why is the subject avoided?

I want to begin by suggesting that we all have a set of assumptions about maleness which inhibit us from even acknowledging that men go through all this. In what follows, it is important to bear in mind that I am not talking about what we consciously *think*; I am talking about what we unconsciously *assume*.

I became aware of these assumptions whilst I was writing this book. It was common for both men and women to express intrigue that I was writing about so 'unusual' a subject. Most assumed that the book would be a practical guide to the financial and legal aspects of divorce. When I said it wasn't, that I was more interested in the emotional lives of men, many people would ask, smiling nervously, 'But don't you find it depressing?'

Here, then, are two basic assumptions. One: maleness is inextricably associated with the 'practical' level of life. Two: if you delve below this, what you will find is ugly, distasteful and best avoided. These are both harmful untruths. To understand why they exist, it is necessary to look more closely at the concept of maleness.

## MEN AND MALENESS

Men are still very much the dominant sex in Western culture. It needs only a few random examples to show this. Men still occupy most of the top jobs, and so make the important decisions in society. Men generally earn more than women. We consider it normal that when a woman marries she exchanges her father's surname for that of her husband; all families are thus named after the male. Without thinking, we say, 'male and female', 'men and women', 'boys and girls'. These may seem trivial examples, but it is in such details that we betray our assumptions about the sexes.

Dominance is very nice, of course. You can expect to be noticed, listened to, and taken seriously. People feel more inclined to make time for you, laugh at your jokes, even lend you money. Above all, as a member of the dominant sex, you can expect to be serviced in all sorts of ways. Women are not so fortunate. They usually have to go through life struggling to get the attention and advantages that men often take for granted.

However, there is a price to be paid for all this. This

becomes clear when you look closely at the roles men are expected to play, and at the roles that are forbidden. Western culture is full of messages indicating these roles; we are constantly being told what 'maleness' means. There are examples of these messages everywhere, in fashion, art, and television, drama and literature.

What do we expect men to be like when they finish a week's work, go home and relax? One indication can be found in the clothes designed for leisure. Go into any high street chain store selling good, cheap jackets and you will find that many of the leisure jackets are in exactly the same style as the suit jacket which most men wear to work. Then there is the 'safari' jacket. The role implied here is that of a big game hunter intrepidly stalking a tiger alone except for a bunch of faithful native guides. Next there is the 'biker' style of jacket. In this role you would have a throbbing piece of technology to get your leg over and somewhere to go to. Strangest of all there is the 'paramilitary' style of leisure jacket. These are bulky, and have lots of pockets, and make you look as if you have just jumped out of an Israeli plane to rescue some hapless hostages. Many of these jackets have metal rings attached. Presumably the parachute was attached to these. There is also the 'sporty' blazer which harks back to public school days, when it was 'all boys together'. These can also imply that you are really a member of a cricket team, or that you're just off to Cowes, or just back from the Olympic games.

The implications in all this are that, when being 'himself', a man is hunting something, going somewhere fast, fighting, running, hitting something, taming the seas, competing or 'being a boy'. The same message comes from jeans (derived from cowboys) and trainers (worn by athletes). Men are clearly and identifiably male only when they are *doing* something.

Remove the clothes, and the message is the same. There

is a long tradition of nude drawing and painting in Western art. Traditionally, when artists draw a nude male it is usually seen in motion. Nude women are usually seen in repose. There is one famous exception: Rodin's 'The Thinker'. Even though he is thinking, this male is seen to be working *so* hard. The impression is that the man is making this effort in order to reach some sort of goal. This impression is confirmed by the title. Rodin did not call it 'A Man Thinking'. He gave it a title that implies: When Man Thinks He Achieves Something Momentous. This is why 'The Thinker' is sculpted on such a heroic scale: the end result of this thought will be momentous.

In Western art it is the exception, not the rule, to depict an ordinary man sitting or lying down thinking, or in a state of reverie. Now, you may think that it isn't portrayed because it is a dull subject. Why then are there so many pictures of women (naked or clothed) sitting or lying down, lost in reverie, thinking, pondering, remembering. It is as if the only way you can depict a *man* thinking is as 'The Thinker', his body sculpted on a heroic scale. Why is 'The Thinker' so muscular? To confirm that he is a Heroic Man, and not just an idle layabout wasting his time. To prove that his inner thoughts are on this worthy, heroic scale, we must be able to *see* his straining muscles as he struggles to achieve his goal.

Imagine a statue called 'The Thinker' depicting a plump, cuddly little man in a cardigan and slippers, slumped in a favourite, threadbare armchair. It sounds like a joke or a cartoon. Yet it would be a perfectly truthful portrayal of Albert Einstein at work in his study at Princeton. Clearly, our inherited image of the Ideal Man thinking bears little relation to the reality of a genius at work.

Turning to a more popular cultural medium, we find a similar treatment. The TV series 'The A-Team' has been popular for several years both in the USA and Great

Britain. Three of the team are men built on the same heroic scale as Rodin's figure. The plot is almost always the same: a weak, misled male, a female or a child falls victim to some Bad Men. The A-Team immediately go into rescue action. They have a truck and many weapons that make a lot of noise. Halfway through the episode there is a spectacular and noisy shoot-out. Something goes wrong, however, and one of the A-Team is captured or incapacitated. The rest of the A-Team respond by making an ingenious device or machine. Just as the Bad Men are about to make away with the team member plus weak male/female/child the rest of the A-Team retaliate. The device goes into action, and after an even more noisy and spectacular display of violence, the Bad Men are caught, the victims rescued, and the captured team member delivers a final crushing punch to the Bad Man who humiliated him.

There is no doubt that this series represents an ideal of American Manhood. The 'A' is for America, and for Top Marks, and for Action. The team represents black and white American males elevated to muscle-bound heroic stature.

It goes without saying that no member of the A-Team is ever seen to be upset or downcast. Equally, at no time in the episode is any one of the team seen to be thinking. Their response to a problem is always action, never thought. When they do exhibit a sign of mental activity, it is shown in the construction of a device which will lead to more action.

You may say that watching someone think isn't good entertainment. Why then has Sherlock Holmes been so popular ever since he was invented? The pleasure in those stories comes from the reader or viewer trying to piece together all the clues in the way that the hero Holmes does. The 'action' here is either a clue or the outcome of Holmes's thinking.

Sherlock Holmes and Albert Einstein may be very clever men, but they are not ideal figures of manhood. In fact neither of them is particularly masculine. Holmes is rather ascetic, plays the violin, takes drugs, is rather moody and is only intimate with Dr Watson. Holmes, one feels, is a romantic figure, but above sex. Einstein isn't very sexy, either. He appears asexual, rather Puck-like. He also has the image of an overgrown boy who needs to be mothered. It was Einstein who gave rise to the image of the 'absent-minded professor', the schoolboy swot grown into middle-age. Holmes and Einstein are both now household names. They have both entered popular mythology as men who spend much of their time lost in an internal world of thought. The price they pay for this is that neither is acknowledged to be a truly potent, healthy, sane, *normal* man.

## MEN, MALENESS AND EMOTION

From these few observations I want to suggest that we all carry round with us the assumption that we are only fully masculine when we perform roles that show us to be actively in pursuit of a definable goal. The greater the goal, the more masculine the man who strives after it. A truly masculine man is most at home in the external world of action. The price he pays is that if he does enter the internal world of thought and feeling, he is on foreign ground. The deeper he is drawn in, the more he feels his masculinity is endangered.

I have, so far, avoided the generalization that men do not show emotion. The problem is much more complex than that. I believe that there are basically two kinds of emotion for most men: those that threaten their masculinity, and those that endorse their masculinity. These two kinds of emotion correspond to the two worlds – internal and external – discussed above. We can see these worlds meet in a passage from *Macbeth*:

Macduff is a soldier and wealthy Thane of Fife. He has just been told that his wife and children have been murdered by Macbeth:

> MACDUFF: He has no children. All my pretty ones?
> Did you say all? O Hell-kite! All?
> What, all my pretty chickens and their
> dam
> At one fell swoop?

Macduff is clearly devastated. The imagery (pretty chickens) shows how this Lord and Soldier is prepared to express his love: he sees them as small, defenceless and vulnerable.

Malcolm, who is the true heir to the Scottish throne, replies:

> MALCOLM: Dispute it like a man.
> MACDUFF: I shall do so. But first I must feel it as a
> man.

How then does Macduff, the leader and soldier, feel his loss? Does he recall his children? No. Does he talk about his wife? No. He does not even mention them by name. He says:

> MACDUFF: I cannot but remember such things were,
> That were most precious to me.

That's it. Then he angrily accuses Heaven and himself because neither protected them. After a mere five-and-a-half lines he puts the loss aside with:

> MACDUFF: Heaven rest them now.

So much for grief.

Now Malcolm urges Macduff in a new direction:

MALCOLM:   Be this the whetstone of your heart: let
     grief
     Convert to anger; blunt not the heart,
     enrage it.

MACDUFF:   O! I could play the woman with my
     eyes . . .

But Macduff doesn't cry, he does as Malcolm suggests. He makes a vow to find, fight and kill Macbeth. Now that there is a goal, and the prospect of some action, Malcolm comments:

MALCOLM:   This tune goes manly.

Look at how the emotions are strictly classified. Anger and desire for revenge are described as 'manly'. Grief is not merely 'womanly', but also an abdication of responsibility. It's clear that no tough Scottish soldier should 'play the woman with [his] eyes'. To give way to tears and grief is to suffer a loss of masculinity. This is why this group of soldiers and leaders are so keen to stop wasting time grieving, and to get down to the fighting. They feel ashamed of their (perfectly natural) emotions.

According to these assumptions, a man's masculinity is endorsed if he expresses assertive emotions such as anger or protective love. These and similar emotions can be purged by *doing* something. If a man is provoked to feel emotions like loss, guilt, grief, remorse, depression or despair, then he may well believe that giving way to such emotions will threaten his masculinity. This is because these feelings cannot easily be purged by doing something. They work their way through us in quite another way, as you'll see. The passage from *Macbeth* shows that these very masculine men fear that if they let themselves 'give in' to, say, grief, then they will be overwhelmed, paralysed, emasculated. They will, as Macduff puts it, become womanly.

These fears, and all these assumptions, are not based on a rational, thought-out response to the world as it is. They are based on an image of the self which exercises its power from below the level of thought. Thus it is very potent. It is no use being logical and asking, 'Why should a man be considered less masculine if he cries?' The truth is he will *feel* less masculine, and he'll try to stop crying as soon as he can, if he cries at all, and *master* his emotions.

It is useful to ask where this image comes from. That way we can get a perspective on it. One clue to the origins of these assumptions about masculinity can be found in Kipling's poem 'If . . .' Here are some key lines that express sentiments that will, by now, be familiar:

> If you can keep your head when all about you
> Are losing theirs and blaming it on you . . .
> If you can dream – and not make dreams your master
> If you can think – and not make thoughts your aim . . .
> If you can lose . . .
> And never breathe a word about your loss . . .
> If neither foes, nor loving friends can hurt you
> If all men count to you, but none too much . . .
> Yours is the Earth, and everything that's in it
> And – which is more – you'll be a man, my son!

Kipling celebrated the British Empire. He was not uncritical of it, but he certainly believed in it. This image of true manhood, passed from father to son in this poem, is really a blueprint of the kind of male needed to run the British Empire. The qualities he lists are necessary if you are defending an outpost of the Empire with native hordes all about you, and a group of settlers who see you as a tower of strength. Then, indeed, a leader must be like a citadel;

the outside walled and well defended, the inside kept in tight order. This is how you must be if you are to be worthy of the name of man. That's because a man's task is, according to Kipling, to take possession of the Earth 'and everything that's in it'. A true man must be able to protect his possessions.

As the dominant sex, men in our time are the inheritors of this notion about the male. It is an assumption that can influence both sexes even at the most trivial level of 'good manners'.

Picture a typical man and a woman walking down the street. He is well-mannered and so places himself between her and the traffic. She links her arm through his, and rests her hand on his forearm, not holding his hand.

This is not merely politeness and good manners between man and woman. By placing himself between her and the road, he is casting himself in the role of her protector. The custom dates from the eighteenth century when a man was expected to protect a lady from the mud splashed up by carriages. The loose arm-link is another, even earlier, custom. The man's sword arm must be kept free. If he needs to protect her from violence, then she can easily slip behind him, whereupon his right arm is instantly free to draw his sword: the sword is worn on the left, of course.

This assumes that the woman is unable to defend herself. She must look to a man, and he must be ready to be a 'citadel', protecting her.

There are many other blatant examples. Why do the Armed Forces not use women for combat duty? The reason is that if women fight and get killed, then the male soldiers do not have a clear image of who they are protecting. It is still standard Army procedure to teach bayonet practice by urging the recruit to build up hatred for the enemy soldier by imagining that he is raping the recruit's sister, daughter or wife.

Underlying all this is the way in which our culture has, until very recently, associated love with possession. It is common knowledge that the text of the Christian marriage service urges a wife to 'love, honour and obey' her husband. Although society now acknowledges that women have property rights within a marriage, it is, in historical terms, a very recent idea. Many of my interviewees (as we'll see) had a big problem seeing their ex-wives, and their current partners, as separate individuals. The law may have changed, but the old assumptions live on. They can be glimpsed in the lyrics of love songs which contain the words 'Will you be mine?'. Romantic love may seem to be worlds away from the concept of property rights, but in our culture they share a common language. Moreover, if a man is strongly urged by his society to make his way in life by increasing and protecting his ownership of the 'good things' in life, then it's easy to confuse the house with its contents, including the people who live in it.

These ideas about the nature of maleness are not what we all consciously think. They go deeper than that. They are what we tend to assume.

## DIVORCE: HOW DO MEN COPE?

The price men pay for being a protective citadel is that it becomes risky to admit to having a vulnerable emotion like, say, fear. If the Protective Citadel is himself afraid, then he may be considered as weak as those he is defending, so will soon be supplanted. If you are to be a successful citadel, then the following emotions are not permitted: fear, depression, a sense of failure, grief, longing for something irrevocably lost, misery, loneliness, etc. . . .

Divorce can provoke all these emotions, and more. So it is no wonder that so many of my interviewees said they found the experience excruciating. It can attack a man's very deepest assumptions about who he is, his maleness, what makes him valuable. There is a very effective way of dealing with this sort of problem: you pretend it isn't happening. The best way to do this is simply not to inform yourself about how you feel.

I interviewed sixty men about their divorces. I also talked to many counsellors and social workers who deal with divorce. In both sets of interviews there was a common theme, betrayed by the first group and explained by the latter: men will go out of their way to avoid the feelings that divorce inevitably provokes. You will find many examples of this in the chapters that follow. To start with here are a few typical observations made by counsellors working for Relate, the national marriage guidance service:

'It is sad that so many men find it difficult to express their sadness or how much they miss their ex-wives, or how much they fear what will happen to them after divorce . . .'

'I find that most of the men don't know how to use a marriage counsellor. I invite them to talk about their feelings. Either they are inarticulate, or they put the blame on the wife or mother-in-law, or work press- ure . . . sometimes they try to use me as if I was a solicitor or a GP; they bring in a problem, and it is my job to solve it.'

'Very few men come to Relate on their own initiative. It is the wives who see something is wrong with the marriage and decide to take action.'

'The most common pattern is that women come to us first . . . often they complain that they cannot get a response when discussing the marital problems with their husbands. If the husband is willing to come along (about fifty per cent don't) then they usually tell me that they really did not think that their wives were serious about divorce. Usually they are very surprised when they hear what their wives say in counselling sessions. . . .'

'I've had sessions with couples when the woman does all the talking, and the man maintains a sort of reserve. Sometimes they talk in a clipped way, usually saying that nothing much is wrong. Sometimes they don't talk at all. And it isn't that they don't want to open up in front of the wife. It is the same if I have a one-to-one session. My male colleagues report the same problem.' (Female therapist)

The common theme in all these statements is that the men they meet have chosen to cut themselves off from their true feelings. The advantage of this to them is that they avoid feeling pain. To do this successfully they have to minimize or deny the significance of what has just happened to them.

This response to emotional trauma really does seem to be instinctive amongst men. Or is it? Here we reach the heart of the problem. Do men behave like this because our Western culture has taught them to do so? Or do they behave this way because men are biologically different from women? Are all those assumptions I described earlier just the product of the way society has evolved, or are they a fixed part of human nature?

This is a debate that has gone on for a long time, and it will continue to do so. It is not enough to say that we are the product either of nature or of nurture. The truth is that our personalities are the result of our genetic inheritance, our inherent drives, our personal experience and our response to the forces at work in our culture. The combination of all these is what moulds us as individuals.

It's with this in mind that we can examine why men are predisposed to feel that certain emotions are alien to their masculine identity.

## FROM BOYHOOD INTO MANHOOD:
## THE SACRIFICE

Most children in our society are brought up by women. Thus a mother comes to represent, to a child, the source of all love, food, security, tender feelings, warmth and wellbeing. Whether a child is male or female it will see its mother like this.

When a little boy starts to take the first few steps towards growing up into a man, he is faced with a bitter conflict. He needs and loves his mother, but he knows he must grow away from her. The problem for boys is that their first clear understanding of 'masculine' is that it is the absolute opposite of 'feminine'. Little boys of between four and ten are intensely aware of the ways in which they are different from girls. Look at a primary school playground: boys at one end, girls at the other. They are, of course, fascinated by one another, but only because they sense their oppositeness.

There is a children's game that shows this well. It's called 'Kiss-Chase'. One little boy described it to me as follows: 'All the girls chase all the boys. If you're caught, then you have to be tortured, so then one of the girls takes you round the back of the toilets and kisses you. Yuk!'

It is very clear from this that how this boy defines his identity as a boy is by a kind of antagonism, even disgust, for what is female. This poses a deep conflict for boys: they need Mother because they need love and security and the rest; without all this they could not survive. However, if they are eventually to become a big male man, then they have to turn away from all that and embrace its opposite:

18

maleness. Maleness and those emotions associated with Mother-Love really do seem to belong to totally different worlds; this is a conflict that goes on constantly in young men as they grow up. Sometimes it is never resolved.

This is a rather simplified view of the way children grow up, but I have brought it in here because I want to stress that men's problems with emotional crises are not due to some innate lack. They are rooted in some very difficult and painful conflicts.

The good news is that our psyches are always trying to resolve these conflicts. Freud said that the process of growing up is one of integrating all the different aspects of ourselves. A boy may see maleness and tenderness as total opposites, but as he grows up, he will hopefully have many, many experiences that teach him that these are not incompatible, that there is a way that a man can show tenderness and still be male.

The same is true of all the men described by those counsellors. They are still convinced that emotions like fear, grief, loss and so on are part of that other world that is non-male, and therefore female. At any moment in life it is possible, if you allow yourself, to learn from an experience that you can be full of grief, but still be male. It depends on you making a change in the way you see yourself.

If you are a man going through divorce, it is not very useful to see yourself as an embattled citadel. The truth is that you hurt. You hurt because you have been injured. Life has injured you. So what do you do?

## EMOTIONAL INJURY

Denial is a useful but short-term method of coping with trauma. If a person has suffered physical injury, one way the body copes is to deny pain that may be too excruciating to bear. This sort of denial is better known as shock. When the body is injured in an accident, it protects itself by going into shock. Sometimes a badly injured person does not feel pain for quite a long time. The body needs to go into shock in order to avoid pain in order to survive: that is its first line of defence.

Eventually the pain returns. Just as shock has a specific function, so does pain. Pain indicates the place and nature of the injury. If we didn't have pain, we wouldn't know how to set about the process which will mend the injury.

Emotional trauma is very similar to physical trauma. The person who has lost a partner, home and children through divorce needs just as much ease and protection as if they'd been knocked down by a car. Both of these injuries need peace, calm and attention so that a healing process can begin.

What if that badly injured person insists on getting up, limping off bleeding, asserting that he is absolutely fine, that nothing has happened? You'd say he was in shock, but you wouldn't expect it to last. Yet that is how many of my interviewees behaved. Their state of shock had almost become a way of life. Moreover, it seemed as if everyone around them, and the society they lived in, applauded this way of behaving, and confirmed that the best way of dealing with injury was to forget about it for good.

This behaviour is not brave, nor commendable; it is stupid. You cannot lead life as usual if you have a broken leg. Nor can you lead life as usual with a broken heart. The best course of action is simply to acknowledge the truth; you're injured.

The real problem for all injured people is getting better. You get better by allowing the injury to heal. You can only do this if you acknowledge that you are hurt. This is true of physical injuries and emotional injuries. The next chapter is about the nature of that healing process for emotional injuries; it is called mourning.

# CHAPTER TWO

# Mourning: A Return to Health

'Mourning has a quite precise psychological task to perform. Its function is to detach the survivor's memories and hopes from the dead or lost person.'

This is how Freud, in *Mourning and Melancholia*, describes the nature and purpose of mourning. Put like this, it is clear that mourning is normal and necessary. Life must go on. For this to happen, the survivor must go through a process that allows the loss to recede into the past.

We associate mourning with death. This need not be a physical death. It is necessary also to mourn the passing of a phase in life. Parents go through a mourning phase when their offspring cease to be children and become independent adults. The same can happen when a religious believer loses faith, or when a political ideal or a way of life ceases to be relevant. Much of the grieving that surrounds figures like President Kennedy or Elvis Presley is mourning of this sort; in mourning them, people are mourning the loss, perhaps, of youth, innocence, ideals. In short, wherever there is change, there is mourning. So, it follows that many of the emotional problems created by divorce are concerned with mourning.

There are many misconceptions about mourning. Usually we think of it as a state of deep funereal gloom, mixed with the bitter pain of irreparable loss. The popular idea of a mourner is one who sheds tears, feels deeply depressed and is rather isolated by grief. It is considered important to 'get over' the loss as quickly as possible, otherwise the survivor will be stuck in this state. Viewed this way, mourning seems like an illness.

All this is not a description of mourning; it is a description of *incomplete* mourning. For a start, mourning is not a state, it is a process. In his book *Loss*, John Bowlby describes four distinct phases:

## THE PHASES OF MOURNING

First phase: A state where one is numb and unable to accept the loss. This often leads to denying that the loss has occurred at all. Numbness and denial are usually interrupted by outbursts of anger and/or distress. Denial often takes the form of manic activity.

Second phase: Yearning and searching for the lost person. This often leads to 'seeing' the lost person in the street, or revisiting places where time was spent together. In this phase, the mourner feels restless, unable to concentrate. Insomnia is common. Again, there are frequent outbursts of anger and/or distress.

Third phase: A phase of disorganization and despair. This begins slowly to change to resignation and acceptance that the loss is final.

Fourth phase: Relinquishing the lost person, adapting to life without that person.

In order to recover from the loss it is necessary to go through each of these four stages. Viewed like this, mourning is not an illness at all; it is the cure.

## MOURNING AS PART OF DIVORCE

This chapter is about the mourning process following separation and divorce. It also describes the ways in which preconceptions about maleness can prevent the mourning process even beginning.

The first thing to be said about the subject is that it was very difficult to get my interviewees to discuss it at all. The most common reaction was to get off the subject of mourning by describing how dreadful their ex-wives were, insisting that they were glad the marriage was over. It was usual for my interviewees to return to this theme again and again; I felt this kind of reaction was somewhat obsessive. Freud emphasizes that mourning is necessary in order to *detach* the survivor from the lost one. With many interviewees I did not believe that they were detached, in Freud's sense. Divorced, yes; detached, no.

In order to understand the problem, it is necessary to look at it in detail. The method I have used here and in the following chapters is to develop ideas around particular case histories. In all cases, I have not only transcribed exactly what my interviewee said, I have also tried to give an impression of how it was said, and how they behaved. Obviously the interview has been edited, but nothing has been altered or rephrased.

What follows is a detailed comparison of the experience of two men. In many ways they are similar. Both were divorced after a long marriage. Both men knew that the marriage was a mistake within one year. Both did nothing about it. Both became fathers and 'stayed for the sake of the children'. There are similarities of character: both have a streak of independence that has led to them setting up their own businesses, working long hours alone and putting a high value on work.

Here the resemblance ends. The process of mourning was

quite different. The experience of Philip shows what happens where mourning is avoided, so that the mourning process remains incomplete. The experience of David shows the benefits and the problems for a man who does consent to the mourning process.

My first memory of Philip was that he was extraordinarily difficult to interview. Like everyone else, he volunteered to help me with this book. Unlike the other men, he said as little as possible and often gave me one-word answers. Listening to the tape of the interview reveals that I did eighty-five per cent of the talking. With all the other men, *they* did eighty-five per cent of the talking. My second memory was that Philip arrived at the interview with a most unusual present for me: matches. He gave me fifty books of matches with the name of his firm printed on the front; they were all arranged in neat rows.

Philip spent a large part of the interview denying that anything momentous had happened in his life:

ME: Now your wife has left you, what do you miss most?

PHILIP: Someone to cook my breakfast.

ME: Anything else?

PHILIP: (*Long pause*) The laundry. I have to do it.

I asked him about the marriage:

ME: How long were you married?

PHILIP: Twenty-four years.

ME: And when did you feel the marriage began to go wrong?

PHILIP: Twenty-four years ago.

Then he smiled. It was an uneasy, fixed smile, with no warmth or wit in it.

ME:    When things began to go wrong, did you
       discuss –
PHILIP: Nothing was discussed.
ME:    Why?
PHILIP: I was too busy (*pause. Another smile*) working.

It turned out that, after twenty-four years of marriage,
Philip's wife had announced she was leaving him, and
wanted him to buy her a flat in the village where her sister
lived. He did so, and she went to live there. Nothing else
was discussed. Throughout the interview, Philip evaded all
my attempts to discover how he felt about this:

ME:    Do you feel, after a year apart, that you and
       your wife are still a couple?
PHILIP: In the legal sense. (*Smile*)

I then tried another tack:

ME:    If your wife remarried, how would you feel?
PHILIP: Highly delighted.
ME:    Really? (*He smiles again, but says nothing*)

It could be, of course, that Philip was pleased his wife
had gone, that it allowed him to be himself at last. After
all, he explained that the advantages of the separation were
that: 'One doesn't have to satisfy anybody else's need.' That
implies that he was enjoying his new-found independence.
Not so, apparently. He keeps the house exactly the way his
wife did, keeping exactly to her routine. The only sign of
emotion I observed was when I asked:

ME:    How do you cope on your own?
PHILIP: I keep up what . . . what . . . she did.

It was at this point (about halfway through the interview) that I began to feel very sorry for Philip. I felt that there were, in reality, a great many emotions within him, but that he had no language with which to express them fully. His tendency to minimize all emotion and deny all conflict showed in other important areas too:

ME: If your business went bust, how would you feel?

PHILIP: It would be a disappointment.

ME: What would you do?

PHILIP: Sell up. I would live on my capital.

ME: Would you have to sell the house?

PHILIP: I'd sell the house and move to P. [The village where his wife now is.]

ME: And how would your wife feel about that?

PHILIP: She'd be highly delighted.

The same was true of the way he described how he felt about their daughter leaving home, going to the USA and breaking all contact with them: 'If she's happy . . .' He smiled again.

I have used Philip's own words and gestures because they show so clearly how much he was feeling; you can sense it under the surface.

Denying his own emotions affects the way Philip leads his whole life. This emerged in three ways. Firstly, because he puts such limits on himself, he sees others in an extremely limited way:

ME: What did your home mean to your wife?

PHILIP: A place to keep tidy.

ME: Nothing more?

PHILIP: A place to sleep.

ME:     Well, what did the marriage mean to your wife?

PHILIP: Looking after me.

ME:     Was there nothing else in her life?

PHILIP: I don't know.

ME:     Do you feel she wanted more out of life?

PHILIP: More money.

ME:     To do what?

PHILIP: Nothing. (*Smile*)

This limited view of what other people were like extended to his daughter, son-in-law and secretary.

Secondly, this group of people were the only people in his life. He seemed to be extremely isolated. Certainly he mentioned no friends. In the course of the interview, I began to see how this had come about. It was extremely frustrating talking with Philip. This was not only because he gave me so little of himself. It was because he actually shut me out, placing a barrier between us, and so resisting all my attempts to understand him. In such circumstances, how can any relationship develop? No friendship, no marriage, can survive a total absence of give and take.

Thirdly, Philip's view of life was extremely pessimistic:

PHILIP: You think people make decisions. Life isn't like that.

ME:     But we all make plans –

PHILIP: (*Smiling*) People make plans, but it all happens in spite of us.

ME:     What about getting married? That was a decision.

PHILIP: Men don't get married. I didn't want to marry her. When a woman is approaching thirty she will marry anybody who is not objectionable to her.

27

My final question was:

ME:      What advice would you give your children
         about life?
PHILIP:  I wouldn't give advice. It's throwing it away.
         Useless. (*Smiling*)

This despair is based on Philip's conviction that nothing
in his life can ever change. That conviction is, I suggest,
based on fear. He is afraid to begin a process that will
possibly entail feeling painful and contradictory emotions.
Thus he protects himself by remaining numb within, and
shutting out all evidence that might awaken these emotions.
The price he pays is high: he is cut off from contact with
others. He consoles himself by trying to convince himself
that even his own paternal love is 'useless'.

I have used Philip as an example at this point because he
was an extreme case. But with him there were certain signs
that what he said to me was not the whole truth of what he
was feeling. Firstly, there is the fact that he came to see me
at all. Secondly, there is his gift of matches.

There was something very odd about this. Philip comes
to help me with my book, then refuses to tell me anything
about how he feels, but then gives me fifty books of
matches. This can perhaps be understood if we look closer
at the first phase of mourning. In this phase, the person who
has suffered the loss feels numbness, which is interrupted
by outbursts of anger. One of the most common images of
anger is that of burning and fire. We often speak of someone
having a 'blazing temper', 'boiling with rage', 'flaring up'
with anger. I think the gift of matches was a message from
Philip which said 'Look, I am angry'. Poor Philip, even
his rage was ordered into neat rows and sealed up in a box.
It was the only language he could find to express his
feelings.

In the first phase of mourning, the function of anger is often to unlock the mourner's other emotions. The anger breaks through the numbness and the denial and so frees the person who is locked up inside their own loss. Philip's anger could not do this, because it was kept under tight control. This is what he was unconsciously trying to say by giving me matches sealed in a box, arranged in neat rows.

There is a certain danger in comparing Philip with David. It may seem that I am holding up the former as an example of someone who 'failed'. David, by contrast, will seem to have 'succeeded'. These terms are not very useful. Philip and David both faced a great many emotional problems; each chose a solution that seemed, to them, the best way of dealing with the problems. I cannot claim that one solution was *better* than another. All I can do is show the advantages and disadvantages of each. It is up to the reader to decide which solution is the most constructive.

I had a chance to see the phases of the mourning process in action in David because we met several times over a period of eighteen months or so. He wanted us to meet more than once because he felt he was changing a lot and found our meetings useful because they helped him assess the changes.

There were many contrasts between David and Philip, yet both began marriage in a similar way. In both cases, their wives married them; they did not marry their wives. Both Philip and David showed an extraordinary passivity when it came to making emotional decisions:

DAVID: I felt there must be something wrong with me because, whereas I would happily make decisions at work, I avoided them with my wife. She decided we ought to have children.

She decided we ought to split up. I think in
many ways she was much stronger than me
when it came to facing reality. I mean
*emotional* reality. Looking back, I think I was
terrified of feelings, hers and mine. I just
buried my head in the sand. I ignored all the
things that were going wrong until it was too
late to do anything about them.

Many of the men seen by marriage guidance counsellors
behave and feel like this. Many of the men I interviewed
were similarly passive, and avoided facing the reality of
their situation. This is quite a common experience, as the
following remarks show. These are observations by several
marriage guidance counsellors:

'Often I counsel couples who have not made love for
a long, long time. They can even find talking to each
other difficult. In these cases, the women are usually
tense, and feel frantic. The men, however, will
minimize their own unhappiness. I am amazed at how
much misery men will put up with before they'll admit
something is wrong in the marriage.'

'Men often put their heads in the sand, and just don't
face facts. There is frequently a block about simply
seeing the truth.'

'Women do, generally, have a higher level of dissatis-
faction with marriage and relationships. Usually they
come into counselling feeling neglected. In the vast
majority of cases men don't notice anything is wrong.
Sometimes they pretend nothing is wrong. I find that
when they do this, they pretend to themselves as well
as to their wives.'

'It is common for a man to be taken by surprise that his wife wants a separation or divorce. He'll often say that he thought it was the usual sort of row . . . Men often have very little idea of how their wives feel about the marriage.'

Like Philip, these men first deny that anything is wrong, then they put up a facade. What interested me about David, however, was that he was *aware* of what lay beneath his denial and his facade:

DAVID:   Yes, my first instinct was to make myself
          blind to the fact that our marriage was going
          wrong.
ME:       What do you think you were avoiding?
DAVID:   That it would have to end.
ME:       But you said before that you had wanted out
          for a long time.
DAVID:   Oh, if it were that easy!

David then went on to describe the 'mess of contradictory feelings' that he was living with.


## LEAVING YOUR WIFE: THE FANTASY

The interviews with David were fascinating because they revealed that he had built up in his mind a scenario about the breaking up of his marriage. This was interesting, both in itself, and because the reality turned out to be so different.

DAVID:   I wanted to leave, but I was scared of being
          on my own. I was terrified of what it would
          do to the children. I didn't want any pain. I

31

felt lost, out of my depth and, basically, scared.

ME: You were frightened for yourself and for your children –

DAVID: No. What frightened me most was the damage and havoc that would follow if I told her the truth.

ME: Which was . . .?

DAVID: That I didn't love her, had never loved her. I thought that would wreck her emotionally.

ME: Were you scared of what she'd do in revenge?

DAVID: Probably. I don't know. I don't think I was afraid of her; I was afraid of all that damage I'd do.

ME: And feeling guilty?

DAVID: And that.

ME: So you pretended –

DAVID: I avoided any discussion of the marriage. The pretence wasn't so much with her as with myself. I knew I was miserable and scared, but I sort of hived it off into a separate bit of myself. I both knew and also didn't want to know about this bit of myself.

ME: So you avoided any emotional conflict with your wife and you pretended to yourself that you were OK?

DAVID: Yes.

ME: How long did this go on?

DAVID: Ten years. Dreadful isn't it?

ME: Not necessarily. It could be seen as a survival mechanism. Did it help in any way?

DAVID: Well . . . yes, for a while. I felt strong in a well-defended sort of way. But . . .

ME: But inside that defence?

DAVID: Resentful. And scared etc . . . Very depressed.

## THE USES AND ABUSES OF DENIAL

Denial is a useful survival mechanism. However, problems arise when it becomes a way of life. Its usefulness is short term.

David used denial to cope with emotions that were powerful and contradictory. He was encouraged to do this because of our assumptions about masculinity. He couldn't afford to give in to them, for then he would lose some of his masculinity. He couldn't cope with contradictory emotions because, as a man, he had no faith that he could cope with them. Indeed, he thought that unleashing them would cause havoc.

Of course, one cannot claim that the situation was created solely by these assumptions about maleness. But they were a factor contributing to the way in which David instinctively reacted to the emotional conflicts in his marriage.

By denying and pretending, David gained the feeling that he was 'strong in a well-defined sort of way'. The price he paid was to feel miserable, frightened, and depressed for ten years. In addition to this, David felt alone because he found it hard to share those feelings. On top of that, he was making the situation worse:

DAVID:   The longer we did not talk about the
         marriage, the more difficult it became to talk.
         The more I hid my feelings, the more there
         was to hide.
ME:      Did the atmosphere in the house alter in those
         ten years?
DAVID:   Yes. At least, towards the end, it was an
         atmosphere you could cut with a knife.
ME:      Why?
DAVID:   I think it was like this: the more I wanted out,

the more guilty I felt. The more guilty I felt,
the more I hated her for making me feel
guilty. And so on, in a downward spiral . . .

David may well have felt 'strong', but he also felt that his
wife was 'much stronger than me when it came to facing
reality'. Like the women described by the marriage counsellors, she felt able to make decisions on emotional issues. I
suggest that she (and they) felt able to do this because they
were able to take responsibility for their own emotions.

Men are used to taking responsibility for their actions,
but many of my interviewees looked puzzled when I put
forward the idea that an adult has a responsibility towards
his or her feelings.

David was one of the few who agreed:

'I think the first responsible thing I did was to tell my
wife that I thought our marriage was a farce. I was
expecting a sort of emotional nuclear explosion.'

I asked David to describe in detail what he feared:

DAVID: I had this picture of my wife lying on the
floor like a rag doll, coming to pieces. And
the house was broken up, bricks and brick
dust everywhere, and the beams splintered,
and the children crying wandering about
aimlessly. (*He laughed*)
ME: And did that happen?
DAVID: Of course not. It was (*getting cross*) just a
childish fear.
ME: But a real fear?
DAVID: Yes, but not a realistic one.
ME: But that is what you feared.
DAVID: (*Reluctantly*) Well, yes . . .

34

This gives some insight into what lay beneath David's facade. At some level he really did believe that his feelings were powerful enough to destroy a whole house. He felt himself to be a kind of bomb.

One of the problems of dealing with emotional conflict is that it awakes feelings, fears and desires that are very long-standing. They date back, of course, to childhood. David is right to describe this fantasy of a wrecked house as 'childish'. He is wrong, however, to dismiss it because of that. The feelings and images are powerful just because they are products of his earliest experiences. Perhaps another reason why David, Philip and many other men prefer to deny and pretend is that they are very reluctant to have these powerful emotions awakened. This is why David dismissed the fear with a laugh and then got cross with me for taking his fear seriously.

## LEAVING YOUR WIFE: THE REALITY

ME:      What happened when you told her?
DAVID:   She was upset, of course, but not shocked.
         She was, in a way, relieved, because it made
         sense of things that she'd been feeling. At
         first it brought us closer; that surprised me.
         But then, after a while, it became clear that
         we could not stay together.

Although David's wife still loved and desired him, David had to admit that he had never felt the same way about her. He had, in his own words, 'married his best friend', and this wasn't the right basis in this case for a good, long-term sexual relationship.

Here, we are concerned with the effect of the break-up on David:

ME: There was no nuclear explosion?

DAVID: There was no explosion, of course. What followed was a process of detaching ourselves from the marriage. There were rows, and it was very unhappy and sometimes ugly, but under it all I think we were negotiating a sort of truce. We were laying the foundations of what would follow marriage. It took about twenty months. We had the children to think of, obviously. Even then, though, I tried to protect myself from the knowledge that the marriage would end. When it came to the decision to move out, we had *both* reached the conclusion it was time for me to move out. However, it was my ex-wife who actually said the words.

ME: And you?

DAVID: I sort of . . . obeyed.

The reality was very different from the fantasy. Revealing feelings, even bad feelings, can have a positive effect. It clears the air. It makes it possible for the couple to trust each other a bit. They may find out that they agree about things. It may be an agreement to part, but it is an agreement, and involves two people as partners. They are not two individuals, alone in their corners, each nursing horrible fears. By allowing the feelings out into the real world it is possible to purge the very powerful childish fears that the situation awakens.

It would be easy to see this delay of twenty months as merely postponing the inevitable. Similarly, David's need to 'protect himself from the knowledge that the marriage would have to end' could be seen as weakness. In fact, he had started the process of mourning, and this takes time.

The decision to part should not be taken lightly. It's a

choice that has to be lived with, grown into and absorbed. This process does not happen quickly; it is very much a matter of 'two steps forward, one step back'. It is natural to take time, have doubts, decide, change your mind, decide again, and so on.

Here is another difference between David's fantasy and the reality of the break-up. In the fantasy it was one irrevocable step, with immediate, disastrous consequences. The reality was that it was not one step, but a long process, and that the consequences were a mixture of positive and negative.

Until David stopped denying and pretending, he could not begin this process of mourning. Once he had done so he was less haunted by horrible fears, and more taken up with ordinary, everyday unhappiness. Not much of a choice, you may say. But ordinary unhappiness is something we can work our way through. Horrible fears can be shut out; but then we live in dread that they'll return. And they do.

The first phase of mourning involves being numbed to the loss, but having periodic outbursts of anger. In the twenty months of 'detaching', David was, as he said, protecting himself from the knowledge that the marriage would have to end – numbing himself. Yet once he had moved out, David began to have a whole series of brief affairs. On the surface, it looks as if all he was doing was enjoying his new-found freedom, and laying as many girls as he could just to catch up on lost time. There was an element of that, but that interpretation ignores two important facts: 'Firstly, I felt utterly miserable afterwards, and did not want to see them again. I forgot their names in a matter of days. Secondly, I made sure that my ex-wife knew about these one-night stands.'

Certainly, David was trying to make his wife feel jealous and left out. This, I would suggest, was an important reason for these brief affairs. He was expressing his anger with his wife in this way. We have here the two contradictory reactions of denial (manic activity) and anger ('revenge') that are present in phase one. David did not want his wife back, but that does not mean that he was not also angry that the marriage was over.

David's original fantasy is relevant to the second phase of mourning, where it is possible to understand it in another way.

The second phase is characterized by yearning for whatever has been lost, restlessness, insomnia and, again, outbursts of anger. David described the contradictory feelings that he experienced:

'I was relieved that I was out of the oppressive atmosphere. Rationally, I knew that everyone would, ultimately, be happier if I left. However, I also felt this terrible sense of loss. At first, I thought it was because I missed the children. But it was much more than that. I felt that the whole structure of my life had been smashed up, and I'd been abandoned. For about a year, I was in a permanent state of panic, could not sleep and felt very lonely. The emptiness of my new flat was the worst; I could not be in more than one room at once and that kept making me feel so upset. It was not like that all the time, but for quite a long period I was in this strange state where I missed desperately what I'd disliked so much when married. As well as that, I got very angry with her in discussions about money, property, maintenance etc. . . . '

The reason why David was experiencing such contradictory emotions was that he was trying to solve a particular problem related to the ending of his marriage. Whilst in the marriage, he was mainly aware of how it did *not* give him what he needed. Yet that cannot have been the whole truth; it was not all bad. Once he had left, David then had to face up to the aspects of the marriage that *had* met his needs. From his own words, it is clear that he simply missed having a home and family. It was that he was yearning for, rather than the woman who had been his wife and partner. Mourning can be seen as a process by which we solve these kinds of emotional conflicts. One way of finding out that a home and family is important to you is to feel the pain you have when it is taken away.

David's fantasy shows that he was fully aware that if he separated, the home, for him, would be destroyed, and his partner would become, for him, lifeless. His fantasy also shows him wandering aimlessly around the wreckage, but as a child-David. On one hand, the fantasy must be taken seriously because it shows real fears. It is important that such fears are listened to. On the other hand, they are not the complete picture. David is also an adult who wants, and can build up, another, better life. He knew, rationally, that in the long term, it was for the best. He felt the contradiction between the two views of the marriage very keenly. They come from two different aspects of himself, the child-David, and the adult-David. Both views are true in their own ways, and both Davids must be taken seriously. Neither must be allowed to dominate, though.

A leading counsellor of the Institute for Family Therapy confirmed this:

'Often the men are the ones who want out, but they'll also feel guilty that they want out. Once away from home they'll feel bereft, cut off from a source of warmth, and maybe their children. The men want and need to leave, but feel guilty and upset and bereft at leaving. Leaving, in fact, is just as painful, and maybe more complicated, than being left.'

I asked her how she went about helping men who face this problem. She replied:

> 'I mother them. I try to contact the child–part of them first. That's because they usually neglect that part of themselves and often fail to voice it.'

One of the ways in which the mourning process heals the pain of loss is by allowing this bereft child–aspect of an adult to have a voice.

The third phase of mourning is the one where the loss is felt to be final. This can only happen when the separated person feels strong enough to bear this knowledge. The denial, pretence and numbing of feeling that characterize phases one and two are necessary defences against pain that cannot yet be born. Once the mourner has lived with the loss and, perhaps, built up the beginnings of a new life, it is possible to accept the finality of the loss.

David found that he could only accept the loss of his home when he had set up a new one, and met friends who provided a sort of support system.

ME:    Did you feel that they were providing what you had lost?

DAVID:    At first, I tried to use them like that. But, over a year, it changed. One big realization was that I discovered what friends were for. Before I was divorced, I did not really have any friends. My wife sort of looked after me, and there were women colleagues at work to whom I confessed my marriage problems. No real friends though.

ME:    How did the new friendships differ?

DAVID:    They gave me sympathy when I was really down, but it wasn't on tap, so to speak. I couldn't take it for granted. And they had their own lives to lead. So there were times when I just had to cope on my own. But I also knew there were people who cared.

ME: How did you cope on your own?

DAVID: By letting myself feel really miserable, actually. I sort of coped by not coping, not trying to forget, or cheer myself up or get off with a girl. In any case that made me feel false and a bit of a dirty old man.

I asked David what he found when he allowed himself to feel the true misery of his loss:

DAVID: Two things. One was that I didn't stay miserable. That feeling changed into another one. Sometimes it was good, sometimes I got aggressive. But I didn't stay very depressed for very long. I might go back to feeling miserable and depressed a few days later, but I came out of it after a few hours.

ME: And the second?

DAVID: Well, although I knew I had never been so rock-bottom in my life, I also had this completely unjustifiable conviction that I'd be OK in the end.

ME: And that it would end?

DAVID: Yes, very important. I knew it would not last forever. I knew it was a phase, like my children went through phases.

ME: Was that different from the depression and misery you felt when you were married?

DAVID: Yes, because when I was married, I felt the depression would go on and on forever. When I was on my own, I felt the depression

41

would end one day, and I'd be able to re-start life.

This emphasizes the role of mourning as a process of change. I saw it happen, because I met David three times over a period of eighteen months. Each time he was different. At the first meeting he just kept on talking and talking and repeating himself. At the end I had a headache, but was still interested. I was exhausted, though. By the second visit, he had calmed down, but still talked about himself exclusively. The big change in the third visit was that he had relaxed sufficiently to talk about his wife, and people other than himself. On this occasion he said:

'One big change is that I've stopped being so angry with my ex-wife because I have realized that she and I are totally different kinds of people. We weren't at all suited.' (*Then, laughing*) 'Now I realize that she is not my kind of person, I sort of like her a bit more.'

This brings us face to face with the function of mourning. As Freud says, it is to enable the one left to 'detach his or her hopes and memories from the . . . lost person'. David's last statement shows that he had gone quite a long way towards achieving that detachment.

Philip, by contrast, was still attached to his wife because he still lived in the same house, observing the routines she had set up. In his own words, 'I keep up . . . what . . . she did.' An important aspect of this is that, whereas David began to see his wife as a separate and different person from himself, Philip still saw the woman he married as his wife, with no hopes, desires or life outside that. Philip could not grasp that she was living life without him.

In the fourth phase of mourning the lost person is finally relinquished and a new life begun. That new life is only possible if the mourner can really let the lost person go. In the case of divorce this means allowing that person to live a separate life and have loves and aspirations that are nothing to do with the former marriage. Philip could only see his wife as the person who was *his*. Indeed, he never once mentioned her name. He referred to her as 'my wife'. David admitted that, even though he did not really desire his ex-wife, he none the less got jealous of her new boy-friend. Like other contradictory emotions, that feeling faded with time. He still does not want to meet him, though.

It is worth saying here that the process of mourning is not something that begins at point A and goes through to point Z then stops forever. Some aspects may never be fully resolved, like David not feeling able to meet his ex-wife's new lover. What is important is that *enough* contradictory feelings are resolved, and *enough* powerful emotions purged. Furthermore, the progress of this change does not always follow a straight line. Sometimes it is necessary to go back a stage, and re-experience feelings several times.

What Philip gained from his solution to the problem of loss was that he avoided pain. He also retained a conception of himself as a 'sensible, logical man'. David's solution to the problem gained him a chance to start life afresh, with broader perspectives on all his relationships, a greater understanding of himself and, from this, the chance that his next relationship would not repeat the mistakes made in his marriage.

There are many ways in which our society discourages men from going through this process of mourning. One way is that the emotions created by loss are seen as somehow damaging to masculinity. When I asked David what pressures he felt of this sort he mentioned two:

DAVID:      First is practical. Most divorced men, I
            reckon, are the ones who have to earn
            money for maintenance as well as to pay
            for themselves. It's really tough
            performing well in a competitive
            profession if you feel the way I did. My
            work suffered. Luckily, my partners were
            very understanding. [*He is an architect.*]

ME:         And the second?

DAVID:      There were lots of people who felt
            happier if I blamed everything on my
            wife. And I did feel like blaming her
            some of the time.

ME:         Was she to blame?

DAVID:      Yes, and so was I. But these friends of
            mine kept saying 'Get angry!' as if they'd
            feel better if I did.

ME:         Did you?

DAVID:      I wasn't angry, was I?

David's male friends felt uncomfortable when he was
obviously upset and distressed. They felt that anger was a
more manly emotion. They were giving him the same
advice Malcolm gives Macduff:

MALCOLM:    Be this the whetstone of your sword. Let
               quiet
            Convert to anger! Blunt not the heart –
               enrage it!

Here we have the main problem for men who are
prepared to go through the process of mourning. It is the
only way to heal the emotional injuries of marriage break-
up, and as such it is the way back to health. However, that
process can make other people very uncomfortable. It is

44

more acceptable for women to exhibit the emotions we have been discussing. It is much, much less acceptable for men to do so, and in this way they can be deprived of something essential to their return to health. Apart from this subtle social pressure, there are other people who would rather a man avoided expressing pain. Family and friends may find it hard to cope. Other couples may find this divorce-mourning threatening because it reminds them that their own relationship could be vulnerable. The divorced man's own family may feel a measure of guilt and responsibility.

After all, if your son's marriage fails, maybe you didn't bring him up right. So the divorced man's family may not be well disposed to all he is going through. Friends may want to show their loyalty, and urge a divorced man to put all the blame for the break-up on his ex-wife.

Many of my interviewees were, like David's friends, preoccupied with who was to blame. Blaming can go on for years after the break-up. The next chapter is concerned with why we need to blame someone.

# CHAPTER THREE

# Blaming, Dumping and Other Painkillers

Each man that I interviewed for this book was first given a list of the topics that I wanted to discuss, then I taped the ensuing conversation. They could talk about as many or as few topics as they wished. Generally, I avoided set questions because I wanted to have a record of each man's unique experience.

However, I did find myself asking certain questions again and again to many interviewees. One of these was; 'Would you describe how your wife felt about the break-up of the marriage and what followed?' Very, very few men could answer this question in any detail.

## WHO WAS YOUR WIFE?

William began our conversation by stating firmly:

'As it transpired, the person I married was a very greedy and selfish person . . . it was obvious to me that it was just a financial arrangement . . .'

William's ex-wife was an unmarried mother. The father of her child had been killed in a car crash. She married William after they had known each other for three months.

After talking to William for half an hour I asked:

ME:        Putting yourself in her position, what do
           you think she felt about the marriage?
WILLIAM:   Er . . . as I said, she was an unmarried
           mother. Er . . . she'd never done anything
           or been anywhere. The thing is . . . she
           was probably yearning for things that
           weren't there . . . things she couldn't
           have . . . and um, er . . .

There was a long pause. I realized that William had
forgotten the question:

ME:        I was asking you how she viewed the
           situation, how she felt.
WILLIAM:   Oh, sorry, yeah, yeah . . . I think she
           thought that I was being tight-fisted,
           whereas in actual fact, I just couldn't afford
           to buy things or do things . . . I just felt
           that throughout our marriage it was a case
           of forever buying things . . . it shouldn't
           be that important in a relationship . . .
           should it? Er . . . er . . .

And that was the most I could get from him. William
constantly spoke about his wife in terms of her being a
greedy, voracious, spoilt child. He found it so difficult to
put himself in her position and understand how she felt,
that he actually forgot the question. That was the only time
this happened in the interview. Otherwise, this intelligent,
good-looking, able man answered every question in a
detailed and helpful way.

There are several possible reasons why William's wife
needed him to prove his love for her by 'forever buying
things'. It could have been her immaturity – she was
eighteen when they married. It could have been the

insecurity of her circumstances – she was an unmarried mother with, it seems, no close family. It could be linked to the fact that her boyfriend had been killed in a car crash. What is significant is that at no time did William speculate about *why* his wife was behaving in this way. He found it impossible to put aside his own views and feelings and look at the situation from his wife's point of view. It was not a case of William not being able to find an answer; he was intelligent enough to do so. William never even asked the question.

Lawrence and his wife drifted apart. He found their sex life unsatisfactory. He spent more and more time with his friends, drinking or going to parties after work. He and his wife did not talk much about the worsening relationship. Eventually, Lawrence began to have one-night stands, and then he had a longer affair. He was worried by the whole situation, but did nothing about it, except continue the extra-marital relationships. His wife also took no action. She did not have affairs.

Towards the end of their marriage, Lawrence's wife stopped doing the housework. He emphasized this fact several times:

LAWRENCE: . . . and she never found any time to do any housework whatsoever. I ended up doing all the housework. The washing would more or less be left for me to do in the evening. This is what I mainly tended to do in the evenings. Apart from phone up people . . . I end up doing most of the housework, you know . . .

ME: Why was that?

LAWRENCE: I think . . . because I did it, and therefore she found she hadn't got to do it.

ME: Why did she leave it for you to do?

LAWRENCE: As I say, instead of doing it, she left it for me. I mean, I said to her, 'Why don't you do one room a day?' She says, 'Oh I'm ever so busy.'

ME: Did you feel that she was maybe saying something to you by leaving the housework for you?

LAWRENCE: I don't know. I don't honestly think so.

ME: You don't think she was saying, 'Lawrence, I'm unhappy.' She couldn't say it in words, so she said it by her action.

LAWRENCE: No. (*Long pause*) I mean, she still thinks I'm coming back to her. I mean, she still thinks it!

Lawrence's wife could have had several reasons for wanting the house to be a mess, and wanting her husband to clear the mess up. She could have been depressed by the doomed marriage, and not felt able to keep the home looking nice. Or she could have been trying to say, 'Lawrence, this mess is your doing, you clean it up.' Or she could have been trying to provoke a row so that the subject of the bad marriage could be opened up. Any or all of these are possible explanations. Certainly, she was showing herself to be a very unhappy and angry woman.

William and Lawrence are similar in three respects:

1. Each was unwilling to put aside their own views and feelings even for a moment, and speculate on how their wives felt. Lawrence's last remark shows he was aware that there was a connection between the messy house and his infidelity. He was not *unable* to pursue that connection, he was *unwilling* to do so.

2. They both spent a lot of the interview trying to convince me that their marriage ended because of the inadequacies of their partner.

3. Both men kept returning to one aspect of married life. William kept returning to the way his wife spent all his money. Lawrence kept returning to his wife's sexual inhibitions. Sex and money are important, but the way William and Lawrence went on and on about them struck me as obsessive.

I could have chosen plenty of examples to illustrate these three points. Many of the men I interviewed behaved in a similar way, although there were variations. William and Lawrence were typical of my interviewees.

This chapter is about how men cope with their feelings when they lose their wives through divorce. Whilst researching this aspect, I found it difficult to separate it from another issue: the fact that many of my interviewees had great problems working out who their wives really were. Losing a wife gave rise to the recognition that she was a separate person.

## TWO PEOPLE; HOW MANY ROLES?

The basic unit of our society is the heterosexual couple. This, for most of us, is the most important relationship in our lives. For most people it is the basis of their lives. Therefore, we make a lot of demands on that relationship, and we expect those demands to be met.

It is easier to see the demands and expectations men have of their wives if we look beyond the words 'wife' and 'marriage' and see it, not as one, but as several different relationships.

Often, a man first notices his future wife because he finds her sexually attractive. Soon, the woman becomes more than just a lover, but sex is an important reason for wanting to be with her. A life-partner is more than just a bed-partner, but men hope they will go on finding their wives attractive, exciting and arousing for a long, long time.

So, a wife is a lover. Once married, the couple will live together. Perhaps they did so before marriage. Whatever, the wife must now be at least congenial as a house- or flat-mate. Usually, it is the wife who is given the job of making a house or flat into a home, and maintaining it that way.

So, a wife is a lover and a homemaker. As time goes on, a man will have hopes and ambitions in the pursuit of his career. In making vital choices and decisions, he will probably turn to his wife for advice. In this, she takes on the role of confidante and trusted adviser. If things work out, the man will probably be promoted and be under more pressure at work. He may well have less time at home. His wife will have to be understanding about this, perhaps seeing his progress in a selfless way. This may put her into a parental role, realizing that he needs to be given space and time to develop. If, however, there are setbacks, the wife will take on another parental role, that of comforter. Like a mother, she may well be asked to make him feel better when life has dealt him a blow.

There is, however, more to life than just staying at home or going to work. Life is fun, and we all belong to a broader society, too. In a social life, a wife is often expected to be an escort. She goes to parties, dinners, pubs, or on holiday with her husband. And the couple do so with the intention of having fun.

If fortune smiles on him, the man may well extend his social life to include his colleagues and superiors at work. In this case, his wife will probably be expected to be a hostess. If he loses his job, she will be expected to commiserate and also to keep the home together on a tight budget. Now his wife is a tower of strength.

If disaster strikes, and the man falls seriously ill, the wife will be expected to be his nurse.

Finally, if the man and his lover/home-maker/confidante/adviser/mother/friend/fun escort/hostess/tower of strength/nurse decide to have children, the wife will almost certainly be expected to bring them up. And if, on top of that, she has a career of her own . . .

One obvious point about all this is that it's ridiculous to expect a mere mortal to do and be all these things. And yet, our society tells us it is normal for people to live in the small unit of the heterosexual couple. Our society tells us, in all sorts of ways, that a man's wife is the most important person in his life. And so, these demands are usually what a man requires and expects of his wife.

Men, of course, have similar demands made on them by marriage. They are expected to be a lover, a breadwinner, a congenial house- or flat-mate, confidant and adviser and father and friend and fun bloke and success story and tower of strength etc. . . .

## DEMANDS: VISIBLE AND INVISIBLE

There is one big difference between the demands made on men and those made on women. From my interviewees, it seemed men were very aware of the demands made on them. They were far less aware of the demands they made on their wives. It is fine to ask a woman to do and be all this; presumably she can say 'No' to any demand she thinks unreasonable. The problems arise if a man is unaware of the demands he is making, and so unaware of what his wife has been putting into the marriage.

This lack of awareness can be seen in the following:

| | |
|---|---|
| ME: | You have talked a lot about what your wife took from you. What did she give you? |
| WILLIAM: | What do you mean? |
| ME: | Did she cook meals, for instance? |
| WILLIAM: | Of course. And I helped, too. I like cooking. |
| ME: | What else? |
| WILLIAM: | I enjoy gardening – |
| ME: | No. What else did she give you? |
| WILLIAM: | Well . . . (*pause*) a child, of course. Er . . . |
| ME: | And? |
| WILLIAM: | How do you mean? |
| ME: | Well, did she listen to you, and discuss problems, help – |
| WILLIAM: | (*Crossly*) Well, obviously we had conversations. You do. You have to. |
| ME: | And she kept house? |
| WILLIAM: | Yes. But I decorated it. |

To William, certain needs and demands were visible; others were invisible. The need to decorate the house was visible; the need to maintain it was invisible. He didn't acknowledge that it requires effort. Even more significant, he was aware of his wife's greedy demands for money, attention and time. He was not aware that he needed to just talk to her, have her listen. Her demands on him were all too visible. His demands on her were completely invisible. He didn't see them as demands at all.

It would be easy to dismiss William as just taking his wife for granted. But I did not feel him to be a particularly selfish or inconsiderate person; he was very generous to his step-daughter, and gave her both time and money. I think the real problem was that William did not see what he was being given because he did not realize he was asking for it.

He did not realize he was asking because he was totally unaware of needing it.

I found that many of my interviewees became exceedingly uncomfortable and often cross if I broached the subject of the ways in which they were needy and dependent on their wives. They seemed to assume I was insulting them in some way. I felt that they assumed that I'd despise them for having needed their ex-wives.

This assumption is founded in the ideas discussed in chapter one. William and many other interviewees believed that if a man is seen to need support, sympathy, encouragement, solace, help etc., then he loses some of his masculinity. In order to preserve his sense of being a man, William (like many men) chose not to recognize that he, like any other mortal, was needy and depended on others.

There is a twist in all this, though. William, like most people, did need his wife very much indeed:

ME:      Why did you get married?
WILLIAM: It came after this phase in my life when I'd
         been working in the North Sea . . . oil . . .
         and I just got to this phase when I'd come
         home after a few months, and I'd think
         'What's it all for?' Because there was no one
         to come home to.

William wanted a wife and family to give his life some meaning. Is there any greater or deeper need than a person's desire to belong somewhere with someone? William's wife must have answered some of these needs some of the time. After all, William stayed with her for eight years. Yet he would not acknowledge that his wife had given him anything at all in that time. The 'twist' is that William did make demands on his wife, and these demands were, to some extent, met. But William did not acknowledge that she was doing anything for him, whilst at the same time he benefited from his wife answering his needs. It may very well be true that what she took exceeded what she gave; but that does not mean she gave nothing.

So William had it both ways: his needs were met, but he preserved his masculinity by pretending he did not have any needs.

## WHO NEEDS WHO, AND HOW MUCH?

ME:      Why did you get married?

LAWRENCE:   A lot of it was because I didn't want to stay at home with my mother and felt 'I want to get out now'.

Lawrence's father had died when he was seventeen. By nineteen he was married. He always spoke of his mother as a depressing person; maybe his father's death was responsible for this. However, Lawrence did not make that connection in the interview.

Lawrence admitted that he knew 'from the start that I'd married the wrong person'. But they remained married for fourteen years. He explained this in several ways:

'I should have done something about it, but it's always easier to go on, isn't it?'

'I didn't think she could take it.'

'Then my son was born, and I thought, "I must do the decent thing." '

The picture Lawrence has given of himself so far is one of a man in difficult circumstances who has made a mistake, but who is quite OK and just soldiering on, surrounded, unfortunately, by somewhat depressed and weak women.

Lawrence described how he 'drifted apart' from his wife by becoming more and more involved in a pub-based social life. Then he had what he described as 'my first minor affair':

LAWRENCE:   . . . and I thought, 'Oh, this is better . . . this is lots better than being at home.'

ME:   You mean you liked her more than your wife?

LAWRENCE:   Yes, the sex was better. I can't remember what age she was.

ME:   What was her name?

LAWRENCE:   And she introduced me to things I'd just read about in magazines and I'd think, 'Oh that'd be nice,' you know, but which were definitely not allowed – I mean, in the whole fourteen years we were married I'd said so many times to my wife, 'Wouldn't it be nice to make oral love?' But no, no. Then, about a week before I left, she said, 'Oh, I'd really like to have oral love,' and I thought, after fourteen years of wanting to, you know, and I said, 'Stuff it.'

ME:   Do you think your wife would have been less inhibited with another man?

LAWRENCE:   No. It was her upbringing. Now perhaps I'm to blame for not telling her what I wanted. But then again I did. I said, 'Wouldn't it be nice to try oral love?' And different positions. I mean, she always kept on her underwear in bed. I mean, every time in the same position, it's like having fish and chips

every night of the week . . . I said to
her, 'It's like having fish and chips every
night of the week, it gets repetitive.'
Perhaps I base too much on sex, I don't
know.

Throughout the interview, Lawrence stressed how inhibited his wife was, and how she held him back from
exploring his sexuality. He mentioned very few aspects of
the marriage other than sex, housework, his pub-life and
how his wife was rather inadequate. He, by contrast, was
holding down a job and, soon, quite a few affairs. Then he
came back and did the housework.

So it seems that Lawrence was OK and his wife was not.
When he finally did leave, however, the facts told another
story:

LAWRENCE:    I told her I had to go . . . only for a few
days to get some space . . . and she
helped me pack. I don't know why . . .
ME:          What happened when you moved out
finally?
LAWRENCE:    I did the wrong thing. I moved out on a
Wednesday, and foolishly took the
Wednesday, Thursday and Friday as a
holiday . . . I should have gone to work
because, with the weekend, I had five of
the most miserable days ever in my life.
The only thing I had was my own
thoughts, it was like solitary confinement.
ME:          Were you alone in the house?
LAWRENCE:    I was alone with eight total strangers.

It is clear from this that Lawrence found being on his own
utterly appalling. Five days on his own was the most he

could take. Moreover, what he missed was an intimate relationship. The house was not empty; it was empty of his wife and home. Only by losing both of these in a dramatic way did Lawrence realize that he needed them. I suspect that he was not reassuring his wife that it would be 'only for a few days'; he was reassuring himself.

So, having been on his own for five days, Lawrence solved the problem by meeting another woman, and moving in with her. He assured me that he and his girl-friend had a 'much better basic relationship':

ME:        How is it different from your marriage?
LAWRENCE:   Well, sexually it's another world.
ME:        And in other ways?
LAWRENCE:   Er . . . we communicate properly, I think.

At this point his girl-friend intervened:

GIRL-FRIEND: It's more adult, Lawrence.
LAWRENCE:   Yes. It is.

I had doubts about this last point. His girl-friend had, in fact, insisted on being present throughout the entire interview. She watched Lawrence intently as he answered my questions, corrected him a lot, and always brought the conversation round to the ways in which his ex-wife was undermining them as a couple. All the time she did this, Lawrence's girl-friend was clutching a five-foot-long pink panda bear.

Most of the girl-friend's remarks shifted responsibility away from Lawrence and on to his ex-wife:

ME:        Did your wife disapprove of you being out so much?
LAWRENCE:   No. Not really.

GIRL-FRIEND:    She encouraged him.
LAWRENCE:      Yes, if anything she encouraged me.

I had the feeling that they wanted me to see Lawrence's infidelity as an inevitable and excusable result of his wife's behaviour. As a couple, they were especially critical of his ex-wife's neediness:

ME:              Did your wife think she'd married the wrong person?
LAWRENCE:      No.
GIRL-FRIEND:    Oh he's still coming home according to her.
LAWRENCE:      Yes!
*They both laugh. Girl-friend hugs panda bear.*


## WHO NEEDS WHO, AND WHAT FOR?

The image of a pathetic, deluded and inadequate ex-wife was useful to Lawrence and his girl-friend. I felt they needed her there to help bolster their image of themselves as the adult couple. An underlying anxiety kept coming out, though, in the way the girl-friend kept reassuring herself with the panda. They were particularly keen that I knew that they had a wonderful sex life, whereas Lawrence's ex-wife was inadequate in this area. One definition of 'adult' to Lawrence was having sex in the bath. However, he stressed again and again that his ex-wife, who kept her knickers on in bed etc., was trying to undermine them as a couple:

LAWRENCE:      She spread these rumours around work, against me. In the end, I had to leave.
GIRL-FRIEND:    And she rang my best friend at work,

and said, 'Are you that bitch who takes husbands off?'

What is significant is not that Lawrence's wife is behaving this way, but that he had exactly the same situation with his mother when he was first married. There again, he protested that his life was being undermined by an older, interfering, possessive and inadequate woman. The outcome was the same:

LAWRENCE:     She never approved of my wife, did my mother. Never. We had phone calls, phone calls. In the end we had to leave the area.

It is worth asking whether these 'interfering' women are as inadequate as Lawrence says they are. His mother may well have felt rudely abandoned by her son at a time when she felt the loss of her husband most keenly. Lawrence did not see any connection between his father's death and his mother's needing him to be with her.

No doubt Lawrence's wife did have problems being spontaneously loving when it came to sex. Many people do have such problems. Yet this same woman managed to keep a home running for all but the last year of their fourteen-year marriage. She also held down several jobs that were demanding and dirty (e.g. hospital cleaning), brought up their son, looked after Lawrence and never demanded that Lawrence stay at home with her all the time. In fact, she encouraged him to have a social life. Unlike Lawrence, she had no fear of being left on her own. Lawrence did leave her alone quite a lot.

So, Lawrence's wife was not as utterly helpless as he insisted. His mother's behaviour was explicable and not necessarily a permanent feature of her character.

The pattern of Lawrence's life shows that he is much more anxious and needy than either of these women. Clearly, he found that being alone for five days 'with just a single bed, a wardrobe, and my own thoughts' was a dreadful experience. Most people might find it a bit boring, or lonely or depressing. Lawrence felt it was 'like solitary confinement'. Later he described it as 'terrible, terrible. I just can't find the words. It was, it was . . .' There was a long pause, and then he changed the subject.

We can see how much Lawrence dreaded being alone by the fact that he arranged his life so that he never was alone. He went from his mother's house to live with a wife. Whilst with her he also had a hectic social life, and later an extra-marital love life. Then, except for five days, he lived with his new girl-friend. Lawrence has lived alone for five days in his whole life.

ME:   Why didn't you move into your own flat instead of going straight into another relationship?

LAWRENCE: Well, it was difficult to find flats. It's not like London, you know. But I also wanted to travel. On my own if necessary.

ME:   Where would you like to go?

LAWRENCE: Oh . . . the world.

I had my doubts about this last point. When Lawrence was separating from his wife, he was made ill by the whole process. Severing that bond of intimacy gave him several bouts of pneumonia.

★  ★  ★

## DUMPING, OR INVESTING IN ANOTHER'S FAILURE

The problem for Lawrence was that although he was very afraid of being on his own, to admit it would have damaged his sense of being a man. He solved this problem, firstly, by never being alone. Secondly, he chose women who were as needy and fearful as himself. They expressed this fear by being, at times, possessive and clinging. They were not like this all the time, but certainly when they felt abandoned or bereaved. This suited Lawrence well because he could both have his (very considerable) needs met, and also blame these women for holding him back from fully expressing his adult masculinity by being possessive.

It was important to Lawrence that he was tied to a weak, depressed, clinging, inadequate partner, because it hid the fact that he was all these things himself. This is why he was unable to see his ex-wife in any other light. After all, if he began to see that his wife could, in many ways, cope with life better than he, then he would have to admit that he was very, very needy. This would be a blow to his masculinity. Maybe those five days were dreadful because he realized, for the first time, the depth of his own neediness.

Like so many of the men I interviewed, Lawrence and William could not afford to see the marriage from their partner's point of view. This was because they had invested so much in seeing their wives as somehow weaker than themselves. If they were to change this view, then they would have to see themselves in a new light.

I listed three of the ways in which William and Lawrence's reactions to the loss of a partner through divorce were typical. These can all be explained by this 'investment' in the ex-partner's inadequacy. For example, if Lawrence had allowed himself to see things from his wife's point of view, it would have endangered his view of himself as being more adult than her. It would also have endangered the view of him and his girl-friend that their relationship was more adult than Lawrence's marriage had been.

It is consistent with this 'investment' that the ex-wife's inadequacies are blamed for the end of the marriage. Furthermore, in order not to see that there were ways in which the ex-wife was strong, Lawrence (like so many of my interviewees) always went back and back to the ex-wife's greatest weakness. In this case, it was sex. That obsession is, really, a smoke-screen to obscure the ways in which his ex-wife was strong, and the ways in which she met his needs.

The advantage of this technique for Lawrence was that he and his girl-friend temporarily felt better. However, they were still tied to Lawrence's ex-wife; they could not possibly afford to let her go. The process of mourning, which is intended to separate the one who is bereaved from the person he has lost, is never allowed to begin. This is because Lawrence cannot afford to lose his wife forever. So he is still 'married', in a sense.

I soon began to be suspicious of the men who claimed that the marriage foundered on the wife's inadequacies. They tended to portray themselves as fundamentally stronger, more sensible, more decent than their wives, but unlucky. It seemed too good to be true. For example, William was keen that I knew he did not go in for what he had been told was 'shit-thinking' or 'negativity'. He was bright, positive, go-ahead and would be a success. It was just unlucky that he was married to a woman who was so immature, greedy and who did 'think a lot of shit', and was negative and defeatist.

I do not doubt that William's wife was like this at times. But then, everyone is capable of feeling that the world is a bloody awful place, that all effort is useless, because nothing ever works out as you want it to. People who are trying to make their way in the world will be especially prone to this kind of negativity and defeatism. They are embarking on a difficult and risky phase of life. That kind of feeling is normal. It is not normal to assert, as William did, that he was always bright and positive. I think it shows how much he feared depression. His way of dealing with it was to see his wife as depressed and trying to drag him down. Once again, he had made a big investment in her being inadequate in dealing with the world. He could not afford to see her any other way or he would have to see himself as being inadequate. Once again, he was still tied to her by this. To reinforce his positive image of himself Lawrence was living in a threesome with a 'sexy' girl and an old nag; William had decided that women were not for him, and had become something of a misogynist.

## WHO DUMPS WINS?

In this chapter we have been looking at one quite common way of coping with the loss of a partner through divorce. This method of coping is based on denial. Deny the wife was of any value as a person, and you have lost nothing. Deny that you miss even the least aspect of life with her by pretending that she never did anything for you, and you take the pain out of loss. Deny you are upset or guilty or grieving by dumping all these 'inadequacies' on her, and you are clearly better off without her.

Paradoxically, this is not a way of leaving a woman, but of staying with her. She must be there in your mind for you to deny you miss her. She needs to keep returning so that you can reaffirm that she did nothing for you. If you are to dump all your fears and depression on her, she must be there to be dumped on. This is why Lawrence, William and many other men were still leading lives that somehow depended on their ex-wives, even if, as one man said to me:

'My life now is so much better because I decide every day to do something that my wife would totally disapprove of. I'm the opposite to her and I intend to stay that way.'

A few minutes earlier I had asked him:

ME:    Why did you leave your wife?
HIM:   Because I wanted to be free.
ME:    Free to do what?
HIM:   No, *free*. Free of her, I mean.


## THE 'CLEAN BREAK', OR DUMPING THE LOT

Another way of trying to avoid mourning is through the assertion many men put forward: that it is better to have a 'clean break' than to allow a relationship to linger on and on. Now, obviously there is no sense in trying to keep a relationship going when staying together is more painful than parting. However, the man that used the phrase 'clean break' (and many did) usually meant that one day they decided to just vanish out of the lives of their wives and children. From that point on they made no attempt to contact those they had left.

In chapter six we will look at the effect of this on children. It is the cause of immense, long-lasting misery for both adults and children alike, and yet many think it a good idea.

Let's look at the experience of a man whose wife left him suddenly, without explanation:

'It was torment. It wasn't so much that I was miserable that she had gone, but that she was, somehow, still there. You see, if someone leaves you with no explanation, and then won't speak to you or have any contact with you, that isn't the end of the relationship. The effect wasn't to make me forget her. It was the opposite. I became obsessed with her, because of all the unresolved questions and emotions left when that relationship was, well, amputated. That's the only word I can think of that describes it. All the good feelings and the bad ones I felt for her were just chucked back at me, and tormented me. It took a year of therapy to get over that. I think I might send her the bill, the bitch. She never left a forwarding address though . . . just vanished. I had all these questions to ask her, you see.'

This man's pain and anger came from being deprived of the chance to go through the process where he could, gradually, give up the relationship in both its good and bad aspects. As we know, the process of mourning is all important: if he cannot mourn, then he cannot give her up. This is why he says he was miserable, because 'she was, somehow, still there'. She was still present because he had had no answers to all his questions. I asked what these questions were:

'Oh, things like, "Was it because I did something wrong? Was it because you found someone else? Why didn't you tell me?" The list is endless. And I wanted to know when she decided, how she decided, what made her decide, why she took all our photograph albums . . . You see, if those questions are not answered, then you go on having these conversations in your head, interminably. That's the torture of it.'

This is exactly why it does take a long time to end an important sexual relationship. These questions have to be asked and answered. The answers must be assimilated by each partner. The reason why this man was tortured by the fact that his wife took their photographs was because he had no idea what value his wife put on him and the marriage. He had no way of finding out the truth, and so coming to terms with the truth. He had no idea what it was about him that made her dislike him enough to go, and what it was about him that she wanted to keep and cherish. He needed to know the answer to this riddle if he was to say goodbye to the relationship and move on.

'But the real reason I hate her is what she did to my sex life. I couldn't go to bed with another woman without thinking of her. If she wanted to keep me, then she's succeeded. But if I ever met her, I'd probably break her neck.'

These last comments reveal one possible reason why 'the clean break' is so attractive to some people. It's the one sure way of remaining in the life of the person you have left. It is cruel and, in a way, cowardly, because the person who leaves avoids going through the process of becoming less and less important to their ex-partner. The one who leaves escapes pain, and dumps all the pain on the one whom they have left. This is why the man who was left said he would revenge his wife making a clean break by 'breaking her neck'.

These last comments introduce the problems of a special kind of mourning. How do you get over the loss of your sex-partner? This is the subject of the next chapter.

# CHAPTER FOUR

# Mourning the Loss of a Sexual Relationship

## SEX: SOME PRECONCEPTIONS

A lot of the men I interviewed had continued having sex with their wives long after the couple had separated. Even some who had remarried told me that they still had sex with their ex-wives.

This simple fact shows that sex has the power to create a bond between a couple that is very, very hard to break. The same men who complained that they found it impossible to live with their wives, still carried on going to bed with the self-same, troublesome women. The power of sex can overrule most other considerations.

It is important to add, though, that many of these men were totally mystified by the way they could still have sex with a woman they wanted to divorce. It was as if they had very little awareness of the power of the sexual bond. Peter was an extreme example:

PETER: It was so weird. We had these rows like, 'I hate you, you bastard,' which really hurt, you know? Then, a few days later I get this phone call: 'Peter, Peter, can you come round? It's that leaky tap. It's driving me crazy, Peter.'

Peter was a plumber. He had left his wife a few months before. He had been consistently unfaithful to her for some years, and was neglectful of her in other ways. However, he assured me that the two of them had a wonderful time in bed, because he was so good at sex.

PETER:   So, I go round, and it's amazing. We end up in bed again.

ME:       And was it good?

PETER:   We never had better sex. Never. But then we get the rows again. So I end up feeling depressed and wound up. Even when we were getting divorced we went to bed. I couldn't understand it. And all this time I was seeing this other girl. She [his wife] didn't know, but I was. And of course there wasn't a leaky tap. I didn't know if I was coming or going.

Peter prided himself on being 'good in bed', but in other ways he seemed very naïve about sex. Firstly, he did not pick up on the way his wife was using innuendo to get him back; he really did think she wanted him to mend a leaky tap, and was surprised that they 'ended up in bed'. He was oblivious of the way he, himself, summed up the sexual games the couple played when he said, 'I didn't know if I was coming or going.' He took all these at face value. Secondly, he really did believe that his wife knew nothing of his new girl-friend. It was quite obvious from her behaviour that she had instinctively noticed the change in him:

ME:       Surely your wife must have realized –

PETER:   No. Look, I even asked her if she thought I had someone else. And she said she knew I wouldn't do something like that. Anyway, I went on having sex with her for four years, and had other women too. I got through a lot.

I was puzzled and surprised that Peter did not see that his wife was perfectly well aware there were other women in his life. It showed in the way she used sexy language and seductive behaviour to show him that she could be as good a girl-friend as they. She succeeded, too. Peter may have prided himself on having a string of girl-friends, but none lasted very long. I suggested to him that his wife was the reason why he had not had a new, lasting relationship. His response was an outburst which, again, surprised me:

PETER:   Now look, you should put this in your book: sex is just sex. It's nothing to do with anything else. You should put that in your book!

I had, without realizing, said something rather threatening to him. I had suggested that sex has an emotional force, and that his wife was able to use the language of sex to say, 'I have everything they have.' Peter rejected this violently. He did not like the idea that sex could make him do something without his consent. However, it certainly did have an effect on him, because we met just before he emigrated to South America.

ME:      Why South America?
PETER:   It's a long way from England, mate.

In other words, the only way he could evade the emotional pressure from his ex-wife was by putting several thousand miles between them. Deep down, Peter knew that there was a direct relationship between the distance he was running, and the power of sex that bound him to his wife.

This view that sex is something entirely divorced from the rest of life is very common in our society. Peter and many other men are encouraged to think that 'sex is just sex . . . nothing to do with anything else'. Every day of our lives we receive thousands of images involving sex. Sex is used to promote and sell any and every product in our consumer society. It is worth looking at the assumptions that lie behind these adverts. As in chapter one, we are not looking at what people think consciously; we are looking at ideas that people absorb unthinkingly, and then assume them to be true.

For example, one of the chocolate flake adverts shows the face of a young woman with sensuous red lips holding a long chocolate bar made of twisted impacted threads of chocolate. She is holding it about one inch from her slightly parted lips. The advert is using an image that evokes oral sex. The glossy lips, the rough yet delicate chocolate are pictured in such a way that a man will associate it with the pleasure of a young woman sucking his own erect penis. A woman will associate this image with the way sucking a man's penis will arouse her. Behind this scene are distant waving palm trees.

Why have the advertisers chosen to make the connection between milk chocolate and 'adult' sex? The reason, I think, is that we have, till now, been encouraged to see plain chocolate as being for adults, and milk chocolate as the sort of stuff that ends up over the face of a five-year-old. The slightly suggestively named 'After Eight' plain chocolates are aimed at the adult market. The advertisers of chocolate flake have decided to use fellatio as a way of making a much naughtier adult connection. It also contains an exotic quality to heighten the eroticism. The distant swaying palm trees,

71

the brown chocolate, hint that this white girl is being aroused by the erect penis of a dark-skinned man.

I would suggest that what the advertisers have calculated is that subliminal erotic and exotic associations will make milk chocolate seem a sexually stimulating food, an aphrodisiac. All this is based on four assumptions about the way sex excites and satisfies.

Consider: the man and the woman are anonymous. The man is entirely represented by his penis; nothing else of him is there. The woman's face is seen in profile, so you cannot see her eyes; thus it is difficult to see anything of her personality. This act of oral sex takes place in a faraway, never-never land, a context removed from the rest of life. The woman's sexual excitement takes second place to the man's. He is erect first, and then, because of that, her lips glow with excitement. So, at one glance, this advert plants four notions about sex in your mind:

1. The most satisfying, exciting sex is the sex between comparative strangers. The advent of AIDS has done little to destroy this idea.

2. Sex exists in and of itself; the pleasure of sex does not rely on the way it relates to the rest of life.

3. Sex really only involves sex organs and body orifices. The rest of the body, the rest of the person, is not essential in sex.

4. Woman's sexual excitement is tied, and secondary, to a man's. Her own desire has no independent existence. In the advert, her excitement derives from what she is doing to him, not what he has done to, or with, her.

The implications of these notions about sex are to be found in other kinds of advertising. The first two ideas seem to imply that the better people know each other, the less exciting their sex life is. This idea can be seen if you compare the way adverts present single people and couples.

In adverts for foreign holidays, latest fashions, Martini, jeans and fast sporty cars the models are usually in their early twenties. This is to be expected, as the advertisers are aiming these products at the younger end of the market. These young people are almost always shown as single; they may meet someone in the course of the advert. If they are in a couple, it is pretty obvious that they have just met. The models are conspicuously sexy. The girls have slim, but sensuous, curvy figures. Their breasts are noticeably full and firm. The men are tough, silent, muscular, broad shouldered, a bit on the rough side, and tanned. Often they have a day's growth of beard.

In adverts for English holidays, family holidays, life insurance, breakfast foods, tinned soups, the kind of bargain clothes sold in up-market Sunday supplements, family cars and DIY material, the models are not just slightly older, they also have very different bodies. The women are slim, with much smaller breasts, and the curves of their figures are not emphasized. Women in their mid-forties and older are shown with bigger breasts, but these have now become a comfy bosom. The men are much nicer, not at all rough. They are less tanned, more clean-cut. Unless they have beards, these men are clean-shaven. These older people are not unattractive, but they are not meant to be seen as sexy.

Obviously the advertisers use older models because the products are aimed at people who are a bit more established in life. These are people who have decided to settle down; maybe they are married, have children and have bought their family home.

But that only explains why the models are older, not why they are conspicuously less sexy. The first lot of models are aged between eighteen and twenty-four. The second lot of models are aged from twenty-four upwards, and are, on average, just in their early thirties. Why is it that these older people are portrayed as less sexy?

The reason is that all these adverts assume that if you are sexually attractive it is because you are constantly available, without ties to individuals, family or property. The way the younger models are presented assumes that the best sex is new sex. Sex is equated with complete freedom, adventure, a little bit of danger, and encountering something foreign. It has nothing to do with familiarity, security, or the rest of the way in which we live life. The implication is that the more you are involved in real life, in a family, in establishing yourself, and in having a stake in some kind of future, the less sexy you become.

It is easy to laugh at Peter's naïvety, and feel a bit superior to him, but he is only stating baldly and living by ideas which we have all absorbed. His attitude, picked up from adverts and soft porn, is the same attitude as that shared by many of my more sophisticated interviewees. These were the kind of men who, after ten years of marriage and a good middle-management job, suddenly began affairs with much younger women. It is a familiar scenario: the younger woman is felt to be more exciting. Eric is a good example of this:

ME:     Why didn't you leave your wife if you preferred Ann?

ERIC:   It wasn't that simple. You've got to understand Ann and I were just having an affair.

ME:     What did you like about the affair?

ERIC:   (*Laughing*) It was the opposite of being married!

ME:     Was it more exciting?

ERIC:   It was the most exciting thing I'd ever done.

ME:    You mean the secrecy?

ERIC:  All that. Secret meetings, messages. Ann always said she hated having to meet in secret. If I'm honest, I liked it. You know, I've always disliked hotels . . . I mean, staying there on business trips. Very lonely, hotels. But with Ann, I began liking hotels.

Here is the same assumption: the best, most exciting and satisfying sex is that which is nothing to do with real life. When Eric's wife found out and threw him out of the house, he didn't go and live with Ann. The affair fizzled out. It wasn't exciting any more, because there was nothing now to escape from. There were several other aspects to Eric's problem. He was very aware that he was growing stouter and losing his hair. This, I think, was one reason for the affair. He wanted, like many men, a younger woman who would make him feel younger. An important ingredient in all this was that the younger woman, Ann, was his way of getting back into an ever-youthful Eden of zestful sexiness. What is significant here is the belief that this world exists, and that it is a solution to his problem of ageing.

More can be discovered about this world if we look at how it is presented in soft porn. In porn videos, the greatest expenditure is not on the actresses and actors, but on the decor and the lighting. A naked woman or man in a medical textbook is not very erotic. Nakedness has to be made erotic by putting it in a certain kind of lighting, and against a certain kind of background. In expensive videos and centrefolds, enough money is spent on decor and lighting that the reader does not notice them, and just gets turned on. In cheap videos, much less care is taken in finding the right sort of room, bed and environment. Real life keeps intruding, as when, in one cheapo video, copulating couples are suddenly upstaged by something on the mantelpiece above the bed: a potted plant which has, in the flowerpot, a little gnome, with his face set in a beaming smile. Seeing that gnome, the whole event ceases to be sexy.

The reason why the sexiness goes out of that scene is that the whole film depends on the assumption that 'real' sex only happens in a place that is like a sort of never-never land. To have real sex is to drop into a twilight zone of perpetual arousal. The sex act only satisfies if it happens in a world without time, an eternal present, where all that exists is erotic. So garden gnomes are out, for a start, and a lot else, too.

This all has a bearing on the rather limited way in which some of my interviewees viewed the dynamics of sexual relationships. This in turn had a limiting effect on their lives. These ideas and assumptions can sometimes have a very profound and hurtful effect.

JAMES: It was sex that kept bringing us back together. We did have a wonderful time in bed; she was the best, the best in that respect. Yet, in so many other ways, our relationship was disastrous. We both got hurt, both hurt each other very much. Against my better judgement, I kept going back to her because of sex. It was just a sexual relationship. But how was it that we got on so well in bed, but in lots of other ways we just were not that close? Not close at all. How can that be?

James had come to see me to describe his experiences following the end of a thirteen-year marriage. He had also recently split up with the woman with whom he'd lived since his divorce. It is her that he is describing here, not his ex-wife. It was clear that actually he wanted to

76

talk about this second troubled relationship, not his divorce.

The first remark that caught my attention was, 'It was *just* a sexual relationship.' Behind that simple word 'just' lay the feeling that somehow a very physical relationship was not as valuable as other kinds. Was there, I wondered, such a thing as *'just* a sexual relationship'? In our society, it is believed that good sex is something separate from the rest of one's life. James had this good sexual relationship, but he still felt impelled to downgrade it somehow. This separation, which seems to make sex so very special, actually has an opposite effect. To isolate sex from the rest of experience is to both overvalue it and devalue it at the same time. As a result, people like Peter or James both overestimate the importance of sex, and underestimate its power as a bond between lovers.

This is what underlay James's baffled question: 'How was it that we got on so well in bed, but in lots of other ways we just were . . . not close at all?' He assumed that if the sex was OK then everything else, as a matter of course, should be fine. This implied that 'everything else' was somehow secondary to sex.

## SEX AS A LANGUAGE

As we talked, James showed that he was, in fact, aware that the relationship between him and his girl-friend had been much more complex. It was not just a matter of the couple being good in bed and disastrous out of bed. There were important links between what went on in bed and the rest of their life together:

ME:      You describe the sex as 'wonderful'. What was wonderful about it?

77

JAMES:    Oh, it was exciting, different every time, and we played a lot, larked about, you know?

ME:    Was it tender?

JAMES:    Oh yes, yes it could be very tender and . . . (*voice shaking a little*) sort of sweet, and we had a good laugh, too, you know . . .

ME:    It sounds as if you felt freer in some way.

JAMES:    Yes . . . I think we did sort of throw off all sorts of constraints. In fact, I often felt she was quite a different person in bed than out of bed.

ME:    Was that true of you, too?

JAMES:    I suppose so. Yes, I think it was true of me.

ME:    So, how were you different?

JAMES:    Certainly freer. (*A pause. James searches for the right word, and then suddenly smiles*) Braver!

James went on to describe how he and his girl-friend had 'a very polite but tense relationship'. He felt that she was unselfconfident, but also resented his attempts to help her by, for example, looking out for jobs where she could earn more. He felt he had to be very careful not to be critical of her. He had to stop himself being 'irritated by the way she'd get very excitable, and say something stupid that I knew she didn't mean, and then stubbornly stick by it . . . by the way she constantly started things and didn't finish them'.

James was a solicitor. His mother and ex-wife were both solicitors. His girl-friend was self-employed, doing part-time teaching to subsidize her work as a dress designer. It was clear that James was an ambitious man, with a strong sense of direction in his career. He had been trained to use language as a method of argument, and the purpose of argument, for him, was to reach a conclusion. His girl-friend was quite different from him. She did not appear to be quite so ambitious, and was content to do a job she did not enjoy (teaching EFL) in order to subsidize the activity she did enjoy (designing and making clothes). Sometimes her happy-go-lucky approach to life annoyed James:

ME: What was it about her that you most disliked?

JAMES: Well, she could be very excitable and giggly and, frankly, stupid . . . say stupid things. And if I said something, she'd somehow twist it in her mind so it fitted with something she was thinking, and she'd start things and not finish them, like books; the house was full of her half-read books. And we'd have to leave films because she got restless and bored. But she wasn't stupid, that was what annoyed me. She was very bright.

This makes her sound quite chaotic. However, when I asked what he most valued about her, James answered:

JAMES: I think it was what we said about feeling freer. To be honest, she was freer as a person than I could ever be.

ME: More spontaneous?

JAMES: I think we made each other more spontaneous. Sometimes . . .

ME: Like in bed.

JAMES: Yes.

What James valued in his girl-friend was a quality that he found both enjoyable and dangerous; an ability to think and act without asking oneself, 'Is this what I ought to be doing?' She had no problem doing as she pleased. In this, she was entirely different from James's mother and ex-wife. Both of them were, like him, trained as solicitors and were, as James put it, 'cool and clear-headed'.

It is interesting that when James was with his mother or wife, he felt that he was 'always out of order'. In those relationships, it was James who was made to feel he was rather chaotic:

ME:       What do you mean by 'out of order'?

JAMES:    Well, my mother and my ex-wife both liked schedules. Going on holiday for example. It was such a drag! Everything had to be put on a list, and the tasks were assigned –

ME:       Is this your mother or ex-wife you are talking about?

JAMES:    Well, both. My mother insisted on doing all the packing when we were kids. My ex was the one with the list fetish.

ME:       Did you feel holidays should be something different?

JAMES:    I had this fantasy of waking up one morning and saying to my wife, 'Let's go to Paris,' then just pack a few things and bingo. I really wanted to do that, just for kicks, you know?

ME:       Did you try this?

JAMES:    If I suggested it, I was made to feel like I was a kid. Or she'd organize the fun out of it.

Here, again, is the tension between a personality that longs to live on impulse, and a personality that finds this irritating and childish. The difference is that here James is on the other side of the balance.

In truth, James wanted to be both chaotic, spontaneous, impulsive, capricious, even childish, *and* cool, clear-headed, ordered, intolerant and parental. There is nothing wrong with this. His relationship with his girl-friend was an attempt to make friends with a side of himself that, with the previous women, had been dismissed.

James's relationship with his girl-friend was something of a balancing act. He loved her partly because she represented something he wanted to be himself. He wanted to learn, from her, how to be more spontaneous. This was why their sexual relationship had its particular character. Through the intimacy of sex, James was gradually learning how to be spontaneous. His girl-friend was giving him something very important, and something he needed and wanted.

His involvement with her was very far from being 'just a sexual relationship'. James was being given something essential for his emotional development. Sex was a medium for this emotional exchange: James and his girl-friend 'talked' to each other in the language of sex.

If we see sex as a language between lovers, then the vocabulary of sex is touch, sensation, smell, taste, sight, sound, words and fantasy. In and of itself the sex act has no meaning beyond the function of perpetuating the human species. We, as humans, give sex its varied meanings. Sex is like magic in fairy tales; it has no inherent set of values built into it; it acquires the values we bring to it. In fairy tales, magic can be used for good or evil. In life, sex can carry a multiplicity of different messages.

For example, Peter's wife used the language of sex to say, 'I can be as exciting and as enticing as any of your girl-friends.' Eric wanted sex with his mistress to tell him that he was young again, and wanted to show her and himself that he was still able to live dangerously. The experience of sex for these men was completely different. For Peter, sex was exciting but puzzling, and even threatening. For Eric, sex was a forbidden, naughty thrill.

Of course, sex is not always a positive experience. The analogy between sex and magic is unfortunately quite accurate: sex can be used to carry and communicate any and all emotions, positive and negative.

81

## SEX: OUR SECOND BIOLOGICAL RELATIONSHIP

James and his girl-friend could communicate, through sex, all that was good in their relationship. In sex, James found he was free of the profession and life style that told him that only a well-ordered mind was of any value. So, for James, sex was a wonderful release.

When James and his girl-friend communicated with words, all sorts of barriers came up. Despite himself, James found he could not tolerate the ways in which she was so different from him. She thought in a different way, she did not listen, she did not argue logically, she had low expectations of herself. In turn, she must have felt that he was judging her harshly, that by making allowances for her he was patronizing her. In bed, however, James could express his admiration for her ability to be spontaneous, for her beauty and his gratitude. Both were skilled at sex because they developed a mutual language of love that was unique to them as a couple.

This is where the assumptions about sex that we derive from adverts and porn are so misleading. These assumptions deny the great variety of ways in which a sexual relationship can be fulfilling. Those assumptions about sex are very rigid about what a sexual experience is. Those assumptions deny that each sexual relationship is, in fact, unique to the couple. This is the result of divorcing 'sex' from 'intimacy'.

James and his girl-friend had problems that, eventually, led to the break-up of the relationship. Sex played an important part in the way this happened. The reason for James leaving his girl-friend was that she went to bed with another man. That act was the result of a build-up of emotional tensions between them.

James had indicated that his girl-friend was not good at

listening to him, and was, as he put it, 'at the centre of her own thinking'. He did not, I think, realize that he was similarly self-centred. I have used the phrase 'James's girl-friend' because he did not tell me her name. He did not use his ex-wife's name either. The women in his life were called 'my ma', 'my ex', and 'm'girl-friend'. After an hour of this, I got the strong feeling that he did not see them as separate people with their own lives. Eventually, I asked for names and he told me, in a surprised tone, that the woman he loved so much and who had betrayed him was called Cathy. Only I used the name after this; he still called her 'm'girl-friend'.

Both James and Cathy tended to ignore each other's needs, and this built up anger in both of them. In addition, Cathy felt patronized, and James felt irritated by her and guilty about feeling irritated. All this was reflected in their sexual relationship.

ME: Was the sex between you always good and loving and wholesome?

JAMES: Well, sometimes it could be sort of nightmarish.

ME: You had nightmares?

JAMES: Yes, sometimes we'd make love and I'd have nightmares.

ME: What about?

JAMES: (*Quickly, curtly*) I can't remember.

It was clear this was a very tender and painful subject. Later, James said:

JAMES: Yes, the sex could change. It was as if the love went out of it and it became er . . . greedy. Just greedy.

ME: And did you like that?

JAMES: Well, it had a sort of thrill, but I'd feel very alone afterwards.

83

This makes clear that, in a sexual relationship, we make contact with some deep and contradictory emotions. In James's and Cathy's relationship, a lot of these emotions were not at all loving. At times, the 'love went out of it' and these other emotions were released: his fear of her swamping him with her chaotic way of life, her fear of being taken over by his great need for her. Great sexual love always has this tension between the joy of being completely accepted and the dread of being gobbled up by the other person and losing one's individuality. The tensions in their relationship heightened this fear, and so the sex could become simply 'greedy', self-seeking.

This fear is, perhaps, what made Cathy decide to assert her sexual independence:

ME: Why did the relationship break up?

JAMES: It was always breaking up. We'd have a bad patch, full of bad feelings, then we'd split up. Then, after a month or so, we'd miss each other, and get back together.

ME: What were the 'bad feelings'?

JAMES: I don't know who began it. I'd start getting impatient and irritated, and then she'd begin to close up. But this last time . . .

ME: Was this time different?

JAMES: She went off with this bloke after a party. Spent the night with him. (*Coldly*) I told her to get out and never come back. I left a note saying she had two hours to pack, and I didn't want to find her in the flat when I got back.

As a couple, James and Cathy obviously had great problems containing all the contradictory emotions they felt about each other. This is why, periodically, they kept splitting the relationship into two halves, his and hers. This final break, though, was indeed different.

JAMES:   She destroyed it. In one night she managed to wreck everything we'd built up.

ME:     How did you feel after she'd gone?

JAMES:   I just wanted to die. I thought of doing myself in. I went and got a lot of aspirins . . .

In order to understand why James reacted so extremely, we must look at the origins of our need for a sexual relationship.

We begin life as part of another human being. We grow inside our mother. Our very first sensation of wellbeing is derived from the pleasure of being totally secure and nourished within our mother's body.

Birth is our first sensation of being separated from security and nourishment. It could be said that birth is also the first moment when we are faced with the possibility of death. Certainly, in the months after birth we are totally dependent on our mother for the security and nourishment that sustains our very life. Gradually, however, we become aware that we are not part of our mother, but a separate entity.

This is a terrifying realization. Anyone who has been with children of about eighteen months or two years old will know that they are very often subject to long bouts of crying and rage. Usually this happens when mother (or father) leaves the room. This is because they are now becoming aware of their separateness from the source of security and nourishment. When mother leaves the room, the toddler believes she has left forever, and is filled with despair, terror, anger and grief. If mother really has left forever, the toddler will die.

In her studies of young children, Melanie Klein describes

85

how the toddler comes to terms with this separateness. Her ideas form the basis of what follows.

There are two realizations. One is that when mother leaves the room she very often comes back quite soon. Mother is no longer the totally beloved source of all life; she can give all this, but she can take it away, too. So the toddler begins to harbour rather more ambiguous feelings about mother. She is good-mother and bad-mother. This could be the origin of the word 'nightmare'. To me it means 'Night-Mother', as opposed to the benign 'Day-Mother'. 'Night-Mother' appears when 'Day-Mother' leaves the toddler all alone in the dark, in a small bed. The second realization is that there are advantages to separateness. When a toddler becomes more skilled at walking, it can go off on its own, and indulge its curiosity about the world, and explore.

Much of growing up is a continuation of these trends. Another important stage is the way we learn how to find substitutes for Mother. It is no accident that children first develop great loves for their teddies at this toddler age. The teddy is a symbolic substitute for Mother. We can go off and have adventures as long as we have teddy there; we have filled the teddy up with all the loving feelings that we need to carry round with us. In Edinburgh Toy Museum there is a huge collection of teddy bears which were taken to the front in the First World War. There, if anywhere, young soldiers needed to be reminded of Mother's love, which gave security and nourishment.

The teddy is a halfway stage in growing up. We are more fully grown-up when we can successfully take into ourselves the love of Mother, and, as it were, mother ourselves. This is why we speak of a grown-up male adult as someone who can 'look after himself'. We are grown-up when we can go off and have adventures without the need to have Mother back there looking after us as we walk off.

We are grown-up when we can be aware of our need for security and nourishment, but also parent ourselves, and so find support from within. However, even grown-ups need teddies; the man who has photos of his family in his wallet is, in effect, taking his teddy with him as he ventures out into the world.

We never lose the need for that intense, close kind of love that we first experienced with Mother. We do not need it in the way a baby does. It is not appropriate for a wife to coddle and protect her husband the way a mother does a child. A wife is a partner, not an all-enveloping, all-loving womb.

That never-forgotten early love was intense because it was a biological relationship. It had a power beyond words, because it was pre-verbal. The language of mother-love is based on the vocabulary of taste, touch, smell, sound and sensation. The experience of total nourishment and security gives rise to feelings of intense pleasure; its loss arouses the most intense feelings of grief and despair. Loss of mother is not just the loss of a person, it is the destruction of the baby's universe. For baby, mother *is* the world.

The child embarking on the final stage of growing up goes on an adventure to seek and find its own biological relationships outside the family unit. These of course are sexual relationships. The significance of sex is that it is our *second* biological relationship in life. As such, the experience of sex awakens all those dormant feelings that we once felt during our first biological relationship.

As adults, we may not need the same degree of absolute security that a child needs. Adults have, with the passing of time, developed other needs based on the desire to be independent. So, if one partner in a sexual relationship does try to create that sort of all-enveloping relationship, then the other partner will feel taken over, swamped; we judge someone who does this as over-possessive. In this case, the biological relationship is felt to be threatening to the equally strong need to be independent.

We would not feel this if it were not that sex has the power to awaken all those early longings for a warm, secure, intensely pleasurable, nurturing love. The power that sex has over us is based on the fact that it can both awaken and satisfy those powerful, primitive yearnings.

The language of sex is very similar to the language of mother-love; each shares the vocabulary of touch, sensation, smell, taste and so on. The difference is that, in sex, each partner gives and takes with more equality. The relationship between the first and second biological relationships is expressed neatly by Sophocles in *Oedipus Rex*. He describes sex for man as: 'to once again visit that place from whence we came forth, howling'.

The loss of a sexual relationship, in the same way, awakens that early experience of separation from mother. James described how he felt after he and Cathy had finally split up:

JAMES: I felt like I had lost something immensely rich and lush. That was how I think of her, you see . . . (*his voice trails off, very upset*)

ME: Like a sort of treasure?

JAMES: Mmm. (*Long pause*) And nothing had much point to it. I remember thinking that the food had no taste. I didn't go out of the house either.

ME: Why?

JAMES: Oh I couldn't. It would all be too painful. And in my chest I just had this ache and it went on and on.

ME: Were you angry at all?

JAMES: I was fucking livid. I wrote her letters and letters just full of abuse. I don't think they made much sense.

The loss of Cathy had the effect of making James feel that life itself had lost all meaning. It is significant that Cathy herself was rather small, and the main impression James gave me was of someone lively, energetic, bright-eyed and speedy. Yet he felt he had lost someone or something 'immensely rich and lush'. He then went on to talk about food having lost flavour as a way of saying life had lost meaning. In these two descriptions of his lost love, James showed how much that sexual love was based upon the all-enveloping, nurturing love for Mother.

Similarly, the loss of that sexual love provoked anger and grief that greatly resembled the reactions of the toddler when it feels separated from mother: intense, impotent, inarticulate anger, and a way of clinging on to the last shreds of her presence by just staying in the house.

This is a normal reaction to loss. I did not feel James was sick or retarded because he was reacting this way. It is one of the characteristics of the mourning process that the new grief has a way of reawakening older griefs. The patterns of our emotions are set very early in our lives; we are always reliving and reinterpreting earlier phases of life. It was not that James's love for Cathy was the same as his much earlier love for his mother; it was that his later, adult love was built on the foundations of the earlier, child love.

When James said, 'I thought of doing myself in,' it was because he had felt, once again, the despair of the toddler when his mother seems to vanish abruptly, taking with her all his security and wellbeing. All meaning had gone from life. Suicide was a natural step. Cathy's loss showed how deeply, how fiercely James needed her.

This great and deep need in James was, I think, what alarmed Cathy. Perhaps she went to bed with the other man, casually, because she needed to experience sex that was less desperately needy. Perhaps she was trying to finish off the sexual relationship between her and James because she felt he was asking too much of her. She could not say in words that she wasn't able to give it, so she used sex to say it. Infidelity is a very powerful way of rejecting someone; the extramarital affair often points to what is lacking in the marriage. In this case, I think, Cathy was saying she needed to feel freer. James, quite reasonably, took this as a rejection of *him* and reacted violently.

In fact, James decided 'after a few days that I had other things in my life – work, friends'. Yet he still kept returning to these early and often violent feelings. Like the toddler, he had to make the hard journey from the wholly negative experience of betrayal, loss and abandonment to the positive experience of feeling independent and strong. He talked of the loss of a sexual relationship, but that was really only a way of describing an emotional loss that was too deep for words, because the initial Mother-experience is pre-verbal.

JAMES: For the first few weeks, I didn't want to see or speak to anyone. Yet I wanted her to know how I was feeling. It's terrible, that state where you can't bear the thought of being without her, yet it's too painful to see her.

ME: Did you talk on the phone?

JAMES: Yes, very politely. After each phone call I wanted to smash something. Also . . . (*long pause*) I found I needed to masturbate a lot.

ME: And what fantasies did you have whilst masturbating?

JAMES: They weren't fantasies, they were memories. I tried sex with another woman, but that was a total failure.

ME: Why?

JAMES: Well, everything about her body was different to Cathy's, and it made me

ME:     How much you missed Cathy?

JAMES:  Mmm. Anyhow (*laughing*), I couldn't get it up, so then I realized I'd better sort myself out before trying anything new.

If 'sex is just sex . . . nothing to do with anything else', then James would feel randy without his regular woman. He'd easily be able to find and enjoy a replacement woman. But here was a man in a state of extreme grief trying to retain the feelings of closeness to Cathy by masturbation. Substitute women only served to remind him of his loss, not to soothe it. As well as this, he was violently angry.

ME:     Did you ever hit Cathy?

JAMES:  I wanted to. But . . . the way I was brought up, I don't think I could. I'd feel too guilty. But once, in one of those phone calls, when she said about this other bloke something like, 'But Jimmy, I just feel better after a quick post-party fuck.' Another of those stupid things she says but doesn't mean, just stupid words –

ME:     What did you want to do to her?

JAMES:  Kill her. Just kill her.

As he said this, it was obvious that James was very upset indeed. When a man mourns the loss of a cherished sexual relationship, he has to struggle with feelings that are both violent and totally contradictory.

Our society does not help a man like James, who actually feels both the anger and the grief. It helps a man like Peter who prefers to avoid all the emotional complexity and to try to replace one woman with another. Both want the lost emotional contact back; Peter got it by carrying on having

91

sex. James longed for it, but found seeing Cathy too painful. Peter was better off in the short term. However, in the end, he had to totally disrupt his whole life and spend thousands of pounds moving to South America in order to flee those emotional complexities. James stayed in England, reconstructed his life and tried to learn from the experience.

When James tried to sleep with another woman he was, in part, being led by those assumptions listed earlier. He tried to pretend sex was nothing to do with emotions, only genitals. His own genitals rebelled and told him otherwise. He tried to act as if the new relationship would be good for him just because it was new. But he found that what he really wanted was the old familiar sexual relationship. It is now possible to see that those assumptions about sex that are contained in so much of our culture are a simplification of the emotional complexity of sexual relationships.

One of the therapists I spoke to summed the matter up beautifully:

'I find that men, in therapy, are often trying to use new girl-friends to get a cuddle. It isn't sex they want. It's a cuddle. But they feel it's childish to ask to be held, comforted and soothed. So they dress it up to look like sex. They use sex to say that they are afraid, afraid of feeling alone.'

The majority of my interviewees said, after a while, that divorce had made them feel, at some point, terribly lonely. Loneliness is the subject of the next chapter.

# CHAPTER FIVE

# Aloneness and Loneliness

HARRY:  The worst bit was coming home and
        finding the place empty. No kids, no noise,
        no one to welcome you. Kind of . . . the
        house felt like it had died.

Harry was describing how he felt in the days immediately
following the departure of his wife. She had left him for
another man, and taken the children with her. He had had
no warning; their marriage had seemed untroubled.

ME:     Did these feelings change in the first three
        months of the separation?

HARRY:  Yeah. They got worse. I got ill. I couldn't
        sleep in that house. If I did, I'd wake up,
        er, I'd wake up around three, not knowing
        where I was. Then I stopped sleeping.
        Then I got pneumonia. (*He smiles*) I felt
        much happier in hospital.

ME:     Why?

HARRY:  Well, there was the nurses. (*Smiles again*)
        No, seriously, I had company in hospital,
        eh?

ME:     Do you think that you fell ill because your
        wife left you?

HARRY:  No. I got ill because I lost everything.

Harry's experience is a common one. The marriage counsellors I spoke to told me it was usual for a newly separated man to suffer from insomnia, or to wake in the early hours, panic-stricken. Many newly separated men fall ill, and sometimes seriously ill. Three of my interviewees had suffered heart attacks, and one began to develop cancer during the first two years of separation. Harry was a robust, easy-going, strongly built man in his late thirties. He took pride in keeping himself fit. None the less, the shock of being newly alone managed to weaken him sufficiently for him to contract pneumonia.

This chapter is about being alone after marriage ends. To be alone need not, in itself, be a particularly harrowing experience. Normally, one might feel bored or frustrated or a bit depressed when alone. Sometimes it is a great relief to have time to oneself.

Harry did not feel he had 'lost everything' just because he was alone. His sense of enormous, deep loss came from feeling that he had been abandoned.

There is a great difference between being alone and being abandoned. In Harry's case, he felt something essential to his life had died. This 'death' deprived him of a basic security: the knowledge of where and, ultimately, who he was. Being abandoned deprived him of part of his identity.

The anxiety created by this situation is not only a problem for the man who finds himself alone after a marriage ends. It is a problem for other people, too. There are two sets of problems associated with being alone in these circumstances. The first set involves how you are seen by others; the second set of problems centres on how you see yourself. I hope that by looking at the source of the feeling of being 'abandoned', this chapter can go some way towards showing solutions to both sets of problems.

## ALONE IN A WORLD OF COUPLES

HARRY:   After I got back from work, I'd wander
          round the house, without much will to do
          anything, really. I only cooked meals at
          home because I felt bloody conspicuous
          eating alone in a restaurant.
ME:      Why?
HARRY:   (*Crossly*) Well it's obvious. They know
          you're alone.

Harry's sense of being alone was exacerbated because he
felt that separation from his wife meant being excluded
from the rest of society. As well as feeling abandoned by
her, he felt that others would see him as not worth
knowing.

One reason why Harry was feeling like this was because
we live in a world made up mainly of couples. Most social
activities are organized on the basis that people come in
twos. For example, when booking a holiday, it is more
difficult to get a hotel room for one than for a couple. It is
more expensive, too. Seating in restaurants is based on the
idea that the smallest unit is two. Images of a happy couple
can be seen in countless adverts for a vast range of products.
No wonder, then, that the man who has lost his partner
feels excluded from a world where 'normal life' means life
with another.

Harry's feelings that he was 'conspicuous' was based on
the fear that others who did live as couples would somehow
despise him. At best they would feel sorry for him and,
perhaps, want to ease his misery. For Harry, to be exiled
from the world of coupledom was something humiliating.

Look at the experiences of these three men:

'My best friends rallied round. They were great. I was always invited round, and somehow they always managed to pair me off.'

'Even people I thought I knew couldn't see that I actually wanted to be on my own for those months. I didn't necessarily want to go out, meet new people, or meet the special person they had found for me.'

'To be frank, my workmates moved away a bit. That was till I met my girl-friend, then it was all OK again. Tells you who your friends are, eh?'

Their experiences may appear to be different, but they have a common theme. In each case the friends of the man who is alone are very anxious that he not only has a social life, but that he also becomes part of a couple as soon as possible. It is as if they see his aloneness as a temporary aberration. In the last case, one gets the feeling that the 'workmates' actually mistrusted the lone man. He wasn't 'one of them' until he had a girl-friend again.

It would seem that the anxiety created by feeling abandoned affects others as much as it affects the lone divorcee. The reasons for this can be glimpsed in this rather intriguing little story. I was talking to an actor who had been divorced for three years:

'My agent rang me and invited me to dinner. He and his wife were having friends round, and would I like to come? Yes, of course I would. I hadn't been with this agent long, and it would be good for us to get to know each other outside the usual work relationship. Date and time were OK; then he asked a funny question. "What's your . . . er . . . status, these days, Frank?" I didn't understand for a second, and then he said, "My wife has a very nice friend; she's a writer."

As I did not have a girl-friend at the time, I thought he meant that he and his wife were doing a bit of matchmaking.

'When I arrived, I found that the other guests were all husbands and wives, married to each other. The "friend" I had been paired with was very nice, but she kept referring to her boy-friend, who was abroad. So, clearly, we had not been paired off for that reason.

'During the course of the evening, the others kept treating us as if we were, in fact, a couple. This was based on the fact that we both worked in theatre. It was as if, for that one night, we were playing the role of an arty couple, even though we'd only just met. It was only when I left that I realized what had been going on. I'm sure that my agent thought that he would pair us off to make the two of us feel better, and less out of place amongst the married couples. However, I think we were also paired off to make the other couples feel better. I began to wonder if they didn't find a divorced or single person a bit threatening.'

I found Frank's idea quite credible. He was a rather good-looking man, and perhaps could be seen as a bit threatening on that account. However, I feel that the real threat to the couples came from something even deeper. When his agent asked, embarrassed, what Frank's 'status' was, he gave a clue. He was talking about Frank in terms of society's view of him; he was not simply asking if he'd like to bring a girl-friend. Since Frank did not have the right status, he was given temporary status. He was lent coupledom for the night so that this dinner party could go ahead according to society's assumption that an individual is really part of a couple. Frank said, 'It was like when I went to Simpsons without a tie: they lent me one. I had exactly the same feeling.'

There used to be great social stigma attached to divorce. These days, we think of ourselves as more enlightened. However, the experiences of Frank, the other three men and Harry show that the lone divorcee can still stir up anxiety amongst married couples. In some way, the break-up of one marriage becomes a source of disturbance for others.

> HARRY: I got so annoyed with our friends going on about, 'Oh, and we always thought you two were a sort of ideal couple.' It wasn't their business. They didn't have the right to look so disappointed.

The break-up of Harry's marriage seemed, to other couples, like an attack on the institution of marriage itself. Obviously, Harry was right; his private life was not their business. Their reaction does show, however, that they invested in a view of life which has a good marriage as its centrepiece. To a great extent, we are all encouraged to share in this view, and it becomes part of the way in which we see ourselves and our path through life.

Our society offers many inducements to the adolescent to go down the path that leads from dating to finding the Right Person, falling in love, engagement and, finally, marriage. All this happens whilst one's friends are doing the same. There are many advantages to this path in life: banks, building societies, the property market all depend on people getting married and setting up home. If one does not marry, or if the marriage ends, then one feels that one has strayed from a path laid down by society and followed by everyone else.

Harry's friends were involved in the fate of his marriage because they all, at some level, shared the same view of themselves, which was based on what they believed society expected of them. 'To be married is to belong.' The person who does not belong is always seen as some sort of outsider. Outsiders inevitably provoke mixed emotions in those who feel that they do belong (and want and need to belong) to what society defines as 'normal'.

Married couples will feel mixed emotions about a divorcee who is, like Harry, an innocent victim of marriage break-up. No one who is happily married wants to be told that they, too, could suddenly end up abandoned. The person who is having difficulties in their marriage certainly does not enjoy being reminded that human relationships can end in bitterness and loneliness. So the lone divorcee provokes both sympathy and anxiety.

On a human level, a couple will feel sympathetic towards someone suffering emotional pain. If, however, that person is suffering from something they fear, then it is possible that the sufferer will be treated as if they are, in some way, infectious. Maybe other couples will help the infectious sufferer to get better fast. But when one man's friends 'rallied round . . . always managed to pair me off', they were not just trying to make the newly separated man feel better. They were trying to erase his aloneness, because it reminded them of the wilderness that is felt to lie beyond coupledom.


## BEING LONELY: A PROBLEM OF VALUE

I used the word 'wilderness' because it emphasizes the anxiety created by having to live outside conventional social structures. An institution like marriage structures your time for you. It structures your relationship with your family, your friends and society as a whole. Living outside a structure is, for some people, terrifying. Harry spoke of wandering around his own, emptied house without any will to do anything. He was suddenly living in an unstructured world, an emotionally blank space with no reference points.

We rely an awful lot on external structures to tell us what to do with our life. To a very great extent, these structures define who we are. Harry had been deprived of being Husband-Harry, and Father-Harry. Being alone meant facing the problem of who he was apart from these roles. This kind of problem faces anyone who has been through a separation, and is one of the greatest challenges posed by being alone.

The main problem concerns feeling valuable. Living in the normal social structure of marriage, one is constantly reminded that it is valuable to be a good husband and father. It is valuable to work hard and have a nice home. The person who does that is a valuable member of society, and will probably feel valued.

If, suddenly, that same man is thrust into a wilderness where there are no such structures, no longer a role as husband and father, then he will have to live with a great number of doubts about his own value. He is cut off from all the means by which he was made to feel valuable. Thus, after a marriage, being alone is part of a process during which one has to reassess the ways in which one is, and feels, valuable – to oneself.

Now we come to the subject of loneliness. At first, it may seem that loneliness is what happens to people when they are alone. This is an oversimplification. Loneliness is actually very complex:

'It's like no one wants to know you because you're not worth knowing. And you're not worth knowing because no one wants to know you.'

'It's not just being alone. It's being empty and sort of lost.'

'In the first six months I felt [lonely] all the time, whether I was alone or not.'

'It feels like being beyond the reach of . . . other people, I suppose.'

I chose these remarks because they describe the variety of emotions that make up loneliness. Essentially, it is a cycle of starvation. One is starved of a sense of one's own value. Inside, the divorced person feels lonely because he or she feels empty of value. It seems that people in the outside world are full of value. However, because the newly separated person feels so valueless, they cannot even approach an outside world which is, it seems, only for valuable people. The person feels empty, hungry and greedy for what everyone else has. The longer they are excluded from the outside world, the emptier they feel, and so even less valuable, and more excluded. To be lonely is to feel permanently excluded from all those aspects of life that make a normal person feel valuable.

This analysis of loneliness is useful because it makes the problem very clear. Is it possible to feel valuable when there is no outside confirmation of one's value? Finding this out can be a very painful and distressing experience. Alternatively, it can be seen as a great challenge.

The phase following the break-up of a marriage is painful – it is useless to deny it. However, much can be learned from it. It is possible to emerge from this experience stronger, and with greater self-knowledge.

HARRY:  My time in hospital was the turning point. I sat for days trying to work out why she had upped and left. It was painful, because I think I'd lost her because I just took her for granted. I'd thought she was selfish, but I think I'm selfish too.

ME:      Did you tell her that?

HARRY:   Oh, she didn't want to know. She just
         wanted this bloke. She's a very cut and dried
         person. Not my type, actually. I realized
         that, too. This was a long time ago. I was
         very young, and pretty stupid.

Harry's reassessment of his marriage, and of himself, laid the foundations for a much happier second marriage, which has lasted for twelve years.

However, in order to feel able to reassess his life in this way, Harry had to feel he was in a safe, caring environment. Falling ill was, in many ways, a very constructive reaction to the stress of the situation. His body refused to accept any more stress, and so got him into a place where he'd be looked after.

One of the marriage counsellors I spoke to came up with a very good analogy:

'When I am counselling someone who is at that point when the marriage is over, but their new life has not yet begun, I often use a childishly simple metaphor. I tell them they have a choice. They can be a chick or an egg. If they choose to be an egg, then they'll see the end of the marriage as the destruction of the whole fabric of their life. It will split in half, and fall into two empty halves. Alternatively, they can see themselves as the chick that comes out of the egg. In that case they will feel small, very vulnerable, greatly in need of warmth and comfort and food. Above all, they'll have a craving for security. As a chick, though, they will grow. A smashed eggshell doesn't recover.'

## JOE: LONELINESS AS ANNIHILATION

For many people, the experience of being alone is something so frightening that they cannot really face the challenge of reassessing life. Joe, like Harry, had been left by his wife. In many ways, their experiences were quite similar. However, Joe felt even more shaken by the experience:

ME: Do you feel lonely?

JOE: Well . . . more. Not exactly . . . um . . . worse than that, than lonely. (*Pause*) No one there, see. The biggest example is like you wake up in the middle of the night, see, and um . . . not that there isn't anybody beside me, 'cos in that respect my wife was . . . well I'll give you an example . . . she would wake me up in the middle of the night if I was sleeping too close, see. And tell me to move over . . . mmm . . .

ME: And if you wake in the middle of the night now?

JOE: I wake in the middle of the night and there's nobody there, not that I want to talk to them, but there's nobody there, um, wake up nights shaking, cold. Had that for a while . . . and the only way I can explain it is that, was that, um, like, like, like a five-year-old child would wake up. Not that he wants his mother, but if he knew his mother was there, he'd be all right, see, but his mother is not there, and he's got no one else to go to, go to, go to, like a five-year-old. As an adult, I know, that is, I'm going to wake, pull myself up, make a cup of tea. But it's like a five, five, five-year-old child, see?

To be alone was, for Joe, so frightening that it affected the way he thought and talked. He was unable to keep to one subject, even to complete his sentences. Every time he said 'see?', he looked anxiously at me to check that I was still listening.

Joe was not talking about merely being alone. He felt he had been abandoned. He portrayed himself as small, powerless, but able to understand what was happening to him. He felt that he had been loved by someone who was so powerful that their love could reach him over great distances. This person had now, he felt, rejected him and abandoned him in the cold, dark night. If a mother did this, in reality, to a five-year-old, then the child would soon be in grave danger. Joe's fear stemmed from this feeling that he had been abandoned in the dead of night by someone who was the source of all love and all security. He tried to be 'adult', but this fear ran so deep that he could not be adult enough to look after himself.

Joe was very insistent that this whole experience was taking him back to how he was as a child. He was acutely aware that the experience with his wife somehow repeated that with his mother. Talking to Joe, I had the feeling that he was not just in pain, but that he was trapped, reliving that bad experience over and over again.

His sense of being trapped was summed up by his house. He had lived for two years in a smallish but potentially pleasant house. However, it seemed as if Joe had just arrived there. It looked as if he hadn't unpacked. The house was not dirty, nor even particularly untidy, but there were boxes of clothes and possessions in the hallway and living-room. Although there were two bedrooms upstairs, they were not used. Joe slept and lived in one room downstairs. It was a small room made to feel smaller because it was filled up with half-full packing cases.

JOE:   I call this my dungeon, see? That's what I call it.

The significant thing about this 'dungeon' was that Joe had created it for himself. He was arranging things so that he would feel more abandoned, not less. After all, if Joe had managed to make the house comfortable and welcoming he would have felt a little more at home in it. That could lead to inviting people round to his home.

JOE:   I don't like to invite, see, because this place
       being like . . . you know, see?

There are two ways of seeing this situation. The first is to say that Joe has created the problem himself. If he could get round to making the house welcoming, then he would begin to make friends, and soon wouldn't be alone. The trouble with looking at it this way is that even if it's the truth, it doesn't actually tackle the roots of Joe's problem. The second way of looking at the situation is to acknowledge that something or someone is stopping Joe from feeling that he can alter his circumstances.

This second view leads on to many other possibilities. It puts the emphasis on the way he is seeing himself. It takes on board the idea that Joe is divided against himself. Let's look at the nature of this inner division.

## JOE: A HISTORY OF REJECTION

When Joe talked about his family, he described the men as competitive. They were all doing better than Joe ever could. When he discussed the women, it seemed none offered him love, sympathy or even support. Joe lived in a world where no one was on his side.

ME:   When did the marriage begin to go wrong?
JOE:   Basically, um . . . er . . . my brother-in-law

was getting, er, doing better . . . that side of the family, I mean, was doing better . . .

ME:   And did she start blaming you for that?

JOE:   I don't know . . . er . . . maybe too, like, 'Why don't you try harder. Alan's got this, Alan's got that.'

ME:   She'd say that to you?

JOE:   Not so much my wife, her uncle, not in so many words, see . . . but, but I could feel that . . . in his eyes, oh yes. I mean, I want to be successful but I don't want to use anyone.

ME:   Does your brother–in–law use people, d'you think?

JOE:   Oh yes, oh yes, I know that for a fact.

From this, it is clear that Joe felt both isolated from and despised by his family. Not surprisingly, he was hesitant to speak his mind; who wants to admit that his nearest and dearest think him a failure? However, whatever Joe's family really thought of him, it was clear that Joe himself held this view too:

JOE:   I was unemployed in 1981.

ME:   And what did you do before that?

JOE:   Oh, I . . . before . . . anything from five-and-a-half years in the Civil Service, Department of Employment, I worked in, er . . . local government, um, er . . . toy manufacture, clerical administration, er, um, er . . . I can do anything. No career, er . . . I'm a Jack of all trades, master of none, see, um . . . accounts, wages, fully employed only in temporary jobs.

Despite being adaptable and hard working, Joe had never had a career, nor very much money. Something prevented him from using his abilities to build a life, and to give him a sense of achievement. It was a cycle of starvation, again. Joe felt he was not worth much, and so did not feel he was allowed to hang on to a job which had prospects and a career structure. He was sure that he would never get very far, so he kept moving between temporary jobs. These satisfied his immediate need for money, but didn't involve the risk of a permanent job where he might not get promoted. However, he was then trapped in a series of jobs that kept him at the same low level of pay and achievement. Consequently, he felt his family despised him. Since they despised him, he felt he was not worth much, and so on . . .

The same repeating pattern can be seen in Joe's relationships with women. We have already seen how Joe described his wife as a woman who rejected him: 'She would wake me up in the middle of the night if I was sleeping too close, see. And tell me to move over . . . mmm.' This was one of many examples which portrayed Joe as a man loving and needing a woman who gave him little or nothing.

ME:  If I asked you to describe your wife, what's the first thing that comes to mind?

JOE:  Er . . . er . . . she doesn't show emotion, doesn't show feeling, er, feeling, er, she does with children, and (*inaudible muttering, sighs*) and something closely related, blood related to her, and friends . . . (*more sighs*).

She also put Joe in a situation where he could not help but disappoint her. Both of them had Polish relations. She wanted to go to Poland for a holiday. This would involve Joe taking leave of absence from work for at least a month. As he had only worked at his office for a few months, his employer would only give him two weeks' holiday. The pressure from his wife made Joe so insistent that his employer said that if he wanted four weeks' holiday then

107

he'd have to resign. In order to please his wife, Joe did indeed leave this job, and they went on holiday. When he returned, jobless, his wife blamed him saying that he didn't need to resign his job and it wasn't that important they went to Poland, denying everything she had said about being desperate to see her relatives.

Clearly, his wife was not interested in trying to understand Joe's very real problems at work. Still less was she willing to help him with these and other more fundamental problems. Love, care, and sympathetic encouragement could have helped Joe to feel better about himself; that, in turn, would have made it possible for Joe to do better at work, get promotion, and so come out of this cycle. Far from doing this, Joe's wife seemed to undermine him at every turn.

Despite all this, Joe still felt no bitterness towards her:

JOE:   I still have a lot of affection for her. Lots of people when they're divorcing, see, they'd say, 'I wish her to drop dead or a bus run over her,' but I don't, I don't, I don't . . . don't wish her any harm. Because basically we both made the mistake.

A few moments before, Joe had told me how his wife had persuaded him that they should move to London. They lived over a hundred miles away, but Joe travelled to London, found a house, made arrangements, stayed in it, decorated it. Then he phoned to say it was ready for them both to live in. At this point, his wife said she was going to stay where she was, and he could live in London. Even then, Joe would not harbour any bad thoughts about her:

JOE:   People, my family, they say, 'You must have been stupid not to see what she was doing,' or they say, 'What kind of a husband are you, leaving your wife behind like that.' But, but, but businessmen they go on contracts in Oman and places don't they? And leave wives and it's OK. I don't think she planned it, I don't.

Despite the fact that his wife was now living in a house belonging to a friend of his, and knowing the two had been on holiday together, Joe still didn't believe there was any sexual relationship between them. Again, his family told him all this was going on, without seeming to offer sympathy or support.

I would have understood Joe if he had said that he DID wish a bus to run over his wife. I would not have been surprised if he wanted to be driving the bus. The only critical thing he said of her was:

JOE:   I don't wish her harm, I don't. No, no, never.
       I don't know she feels the same, otherwise she'd
       come and see me as a friend. But she doesn't.
       My wife . . . I wouldn't say she was selfish . . .
       but she would think of herself first.

There are many examples of his wife's selfishness: refusing to go to his best friend's funeral, refusing to discuss why she wanted a divorce, and many, many, smaller instances. Why was Joe so reticent about portraying this woman in a bad light after she had done him so much harm?

The answer is, I think, to be found in Joe's own family. He described his mother as follows:

JOE:   Some people, they say it's bad to be an orphan,
       but my family, my mother . . . It'd been better,
       see, if I'd been orphaned and in an orphanage.
       Oh, she's a witch. I wouldn't go home there.

He gave an example of his mother's coldness towards him. It was the first Christmas after Joe had been separated from his wife:

JOE: And she says, 'I told you so, I told you.' She never liked my wife, never. And, I'll tell you this, at the Christmas lunch she says, 'I bet you feel better now you're on your own.' But it wasn't true. It was the worst Christmas of my life.

His father offered Joe little support:

JOE: My father, he says to ignore her. But I can't. And he said to me, 'You'd go back to her, wouldn't you?' My wife. But I wouldn't. But my father, he said, 'You'd go back to her and you'd be a FOOL.'

The first point I want to make is that Joe's relationship with his wife was a precise repeat of the relationship he had with his mother and, indeed, his whole family. In this relationship, Joe was the one offering and needing love. Despite his efforts he was never loved in return, he was attacked and despised when he was obviously suffering. The key question is why Joe put up with this. He still thought well of his wife. He may have called his mother 'a witch', but he was still victimized by her. Why?

## THE INTERNAL PARENT

The answer lies in the way we learn about love from our first experiences of being loved by our mother and father. A young baby does not only take in milk from its mother.

110

The baby is fed by its mother's love as much as by her milk. The process of feeding and nourishment is vital to the baby's survival, and this applies both physically and emotionally. This is because the baby relies, for its survival, on a powerful bond with its only source of food and security. The baby internalizes its mother's love, so that it becomes a permanent source of emotional nourishment to tide it over the periods when the mother is not there physically. This creation of an Internal Parent is the beginning of a love relationship, and provides the model for all subsequent emotional development. This idea of 'internalizing' a parental relationship was developed by Melanie Klein. It was the result of many years of observing and analysing both children and adults.

Klein's belief is that the Internal Mother is created out of the relationship between mother and baby. It is not an objective picture of the parent herself, but a character created out of the baby's response to the mother's personality. If the mother behaves in a certain way, the baby internalizes this behaviour, and then comes to expect that behaviour in the mother and in others. The Internal Parent thus becomes a powerful character within the baby. The baby needs to know how to behave in order to elicit the love and food it needs in order to survive. The Internal Parent, created out of expectations learned from the mother's behaviour, becomes the voice telling the baby how to behave.

If the mother herself is loving and understanding and tolerates the times when the baby is being difficult, then the baby comes to expect understanding, toleration and unconditional love. The mother will, inevitably, be tired and irritable sometimes, and the baby will learn that there are also limits to toleration. However, the baby internalizes a parent who, in general, understands and loves. The baby will then expect that from others. As it grows up, it will approach all its subsequent social and love relationships with the same expectations, because its Internal Mother is a voice saying, 'Yes, there will be limits, but in general, people will love you for yourself.' When the child grows up it learns to parent itself in this way.

The problems arise when a baby internalizes a parent who finds it difficult to offer toleration, understanding and love. The same process happens, but this time the baby internalizes a parent who has a much more negative voice. Joe's early relationship with his mother resulted in an Internal Parent who said to him, 'You disappoint me. You are less important to me than myself. Everyone else will agree with me that you are of little or no value.'

Joe's problem was that he still believed this voice. This can be seen in his description of waking up in the night. He was talking about himself as an adult, but this can be traced back to a much earlier experience. Isolated, Joe found himself alone with a mother who rejected him. His marriage was, as we have seen, a repeat of his experience with his mother. This was because Joe unconsciously chose a woman who would match up with the Internal Parent who told him that this kind of relationship was what Joe was going to have for the rest of his life.

This is why Joe was a man divided against himself. Obviously he did not *want* to be rejected and miserable. One part of him rebelled against this and thought it unfair. However, another part of him was pushing him, against his will, into situations where this rejection was inevitable. We do not necessarily choose relationships that make us happy; we sometimes choose relationships we recognize, where the pattern of behaviour is familiar. This pattern is dictated by the Internal Parent. We carry on the original mother–child relationship.

Joe had to placate or think well of the woman whom he felt fated to love. If he didn't, he feared he might lose her altogether. Even though he was rejected, he was nevertheless drawn back to her because he still needed some sort of relationship. If this was the only one possible, then Joe felt he must put up with it. The great unfairness in all this is that if Joe had been loved for himself, he would have found it easier to look beyond a relationship in which he was constantly rejected. If his Internal Parent had been saying, 'in general, people will love you for yourself', then he'd have been able to say to his wife, 'Treat me better, because I deserve better.' The cycle of deprivation was difficult to escape from because it deprived Joe of the very support he needed to escape it.

I began this chapter by saying it was about being alone. That needs to be rephrased now. The problem is not being alone, but who you are left alone with. We are never fully alone; there is always some internal figure or figures with us. The challenge of being alone at the end of a relationship is the chance it gives us to consider what kind of figures and voices we have inside ourself, and how they advise us.

Harry felt much more secure than Joe. Although he was devastated, and although he felt outside the normal pattern of social relationships, he still felt secure enough to trust that, if he fell ill, he would be looked after. Taking the analogy of the chick and the egg, Harry felt that if he was reduced to the level of a helpless, vulnerable frightened weak organism, then someone, somewhere, would look after him. It is interesting that he thought of the nurses first; they are usually female. He could have mentioned a male GP or consultant, but the first caring figures that came to his mind were female nurses. This enabled Harry to regress temporarily, feel cared for, and then to put his life back together.

Joe could not have such a trusting attitude to life. He could only expect to be ignored and rejected. Joe's solution to the problem was drastic and could have been tragic. As I was about to leave, he said, 'Oh, by the way, see, I tried to take my life last Christmas.'

Naturally, I did not go, and we discussed this further. All through, Joe had kept checking that I was still listening to him every time he said 'see?'. Now, however, he lost all his nervousness and hesitant speech. He told me that he had felt totally friendless and alone, isolated in London, his friends and family over a hundred miles away. He phoned his brother, who proceeded to tell him off for being cowardly and lazy. Joe decided he just wanted to go to sleep forever. So he put the phone down and took an overdose of every pill he could find in the local shop. As he was drifting off, he realized he had not phoned work to tell them he wouldn't be in. His slurred speech and rambling sentences alerted the girl on the switchboard, who phoned for an ambulance.

There are many ways to view an attempted suicide. Joe's case was both the 'cry for help' and an attempt to kill the internal figure who was telling him he was of no value. To sleep forever was certainly one way of shutting up his Internal Parent.

Happily, Joe was taken to a hospital where psychiatric and social care was available. He still did not trust them much, and did not want to join a singles club where he might meet people who would 'use' him. This interview was one case where our meeting was helpful beyond the writing of this book. I was able to put Joe in touch with organizations that would help him.

Being alone is a trial and a challenge. You are faced with the question, 'Who am I apart from the roles given me by society?' That question leads to considering the nature of your inner figures and voices. Sometimes it is possible to change these by using the time spent alone to think and question oneself and one's habitual reactions. In other more problematical cases it is a good idea to seek out counselling or therapy to help yourself deal with this challenge. It is possible for someone like Joe to reconsider and change the nature of his Internal Parent. This requires a lot of work and patience, but it is rewarding in the long term. In Joe's case it was necessary that he work on this problem with a good therapist. The appendix contains a list of helpful organizations who will offer advice and contacts if you feel you need that sort of help.

It would be quite wrong to end this chapter on a negative note. Many of my interviewees came to see being alone as a useful and necessary stage in their post-marriage life. Here, for example, is Ray, who had split up from his wife eight months before:

RAY: I kept having to go back to her. And it wasn't because I wanted to go back; it was 'cos I couldn't bear being on my own.

As we talked, it transpired that the reason Ray had found being on his own so difficult was because he did not know how to organize a social life for himself.

RAY: My wife had always done that, see. For us both.

This became a familiar comment. Ray was in his early fifties. In this age group, and sometimes in younger men, it turned out that their wives had taken care of things like family birthdays, parties, organizing Christmas. A lot of men came to the realization that they had needed their wives to maintain their own social and family connections. So when the couple separated, the men found they didn't have the skill of setting up and keeping a social life. Ray, like many others, found that he had to learn it for himself.

RAY: It was much easier when I joined the club. [Ray was keen on golf.] But still I found I was having

115

to remind myself to fix up to meet my friends.
I realized it was work to organize your life!

The good aspect of this was that Ray changed from being someone who could not cope with being alone to a man who found that living on his own gave him, for the first time, an element of choice in how he led his social life.

RAY:   I think it was 'cos I'd always been looked after. There'd always been a girl-friend or m'wife to say what we'd do tonight, you know . . . But it's amazing that I didn't want to live like this before.

ME:    You prefer it?

RAY:   Look, I can be with friends if I want, or I can slop around the flat if I want; it's a choice. I can choose.

Ray's profession – he was a taxi-driver – meant that he was used to working on his own. It was not that hard for him to learn to use the same degree of self-reliance in his social life, too. Others may find it a little harder.

One of the marriage guidance therapists who helped me with this book discussed this idea that you can learn a lot about yourself when you live alone:

'When couples split up, I feel it is not necessarily a good idea for the husband and wife to go straight into another relationship. I think that each needs time alone. They need time in which to be quiet and to listen to themselves, as it were.

'This time alone is a very good opportunity to find out about what you need from a relationship. When a marriage dies, it's because husband and wife were not fulfilling each other's needs. Often they say things like,

"She wasn't the person I married any more." That's a sign that the couple have grown away from each other.

'Now, if the husband and wife have changed somehow, then they need time to sort out for themselves what their new self needs, and you can't do that if you've got to go through the stresses and strains of setting up home with a new lover.

'I always say to my clients, take some time alone for yourself, think about yourself and who you are and what you need. I believe it's essential.'

Harry and Joe experienced being 'alone' as something dreadful, a period of agony. That is to muddle Being Alone with Loneliness. They are not at all the same thing. Loneliness is a cycle of starvation that begins with the feeling that you have been abandoned by someone who has taken away all love, warmth and sense of belonging. You need to find another source of love, and allow it to nurture you, building a new sense of your own value.

Being alone, however, is a choice. It can be very positive: a period of calm in which you take stock of your life and learn about yourself. Sometimes people decide they like to have a place that is their own, where they can live life as they please. That way of being alone can be seen as a base from which you can organize the rest of your life. Other people need to be alone so that they can consider the various choices life now offers. Being alone is then a period in which you take time and space in order to consider how you want to spend your life, and with whom.

At first it will feel that the absence of those who filled your life dominates all your thoughts and feelings. That phase will pass. Once the pain of immediate loss has lessened, you will find it easier to stand back from the experience and look at what you had, and judge for yourself what aspects of your former life made you feel good. It is at this point that the experience of loss becomes extremely useful. The pain of loss tells you what you valued. That may not have been so obvious to you when the valuable aspects of life seemed hopelessly entangled with aspects that frustrated or hurt you. Once you can feel what really was valuable, you will have learned that, next time round, you must seek out that quality in a relationship.

The same applies to the aspects of a relationship that made you unhappy. The sense of relief that you'll get when this goes out of your life will be a sure indication that it is something you should avoid in the future.

All these discoveries can only be made if you are in an environment that is peaceful, calm and allows you time for reverie. Living alone during this period can help create this kind of haven. You'll need to live in a way that puts no pressure on you, and allows you to get through these emotional phases. Living with others may bring the comforts of company, but it may also restrict you. Others may find that they are made uncomfortable by you fully experiencing your sense of loss. You, in turn, may cover it up to make them feel better.

Only you can judge how you want to live. What is certain is that, in this phase of life, a certain amount of being alone is necessary and useful.

# CHAPTER SIX

# The Divorced Father

ADRIAN:   So, when I knew that the marriage was dead, I tried to work out what to do for the best – for my kids, that is. I decided a clean break was the best thing I could do for them.

## THE CLEAN BREAK

I interviewed several men who made what they called a 'clean break' from wife and children. A few had done it because they wanted to escape intolerable emotional and/or financial pressures. Many of this group assumed that if they did not see their children, they would not have to pay maintenance.

Others had been advised by solicitors that the best and cheapest way to end a marriage was to make a single payment to their wives and then cut all emotional and financial ties with the family. The solicitors' reasons were that it was 'the least messy' way of dealing with the problem, a way of 'minimizing bad feelings'.

Adrian was unique in the group of men who had made a 'clean break'. He was not trying to escape responsibility – he paid his ex-wife maintenance for fifteen years. He was not looking for an easy way out – he felt it was very difficult to break all ties with children he loved. He genuinely felt a clean break would be healthy. I asked him why:

ADRIAN: Because children need to feel loyalty to a parent and not to be confused in that loyalty. I'd seen so many situations where kids were parcelled out – weekdays with mother, every other weekend with father. They just get confused and upset. Mother and father both saying 'love me'. The kids can't; their loyalties are divided.

ME: You don't believe children can feel loyalty and love for both parents even if they are separated?

ADRIAN: No.

ME: They can't work it out for themselves?

ADRIAN: No. Look, I decided my kids needed to feel home with their mother . . . me visiting, maybe missing a visit, would confuse all that. So even if they think I'm a shit for leaving, that's OK, I don't mind, because the whole situation is clear.

ME: But you're not a shit. It's not the truth.

ADRIAN: No, but the situation is clear for them, and that's what matters. It's simple for them.

ME: And do you still feel you were right?

ADRIAN: (*After some hesitation*) Yes.

As the interview went on, it became clear that the situation was not at all 'simple'. Adrian's daughter tried to contact him, and when she found him this created new tensions with his ex-wife. Altogether, his daughter coped better than his son did.

ADRIAN: I don't talk about my son. If someone asks me about my kids I talk about her, not him.

ME: How did he cope with the clean break?

ADRIAN: Well, he had a bad time at school. He's bright. He fell behind. The teachers said he 'underachieved'. He went to a special school for kids who had problems . . . with the police. I think he got on the wrong side of the law.

ME: Has he been to see you?

ADRIAN: He says if he ever met me, he'd stick a knife in me.

The 'clean break' is supposed to get all the 'bad' 'messy' feelings out of the way in one go. The theory is that once the break is made, parents and children will be better able to get on with their lives. It's an attractive notion and there is no doubt that Adrian believed he was doing the right thing, even though it hurt him to lose his children. However, the 'clean break' doesn't work, as the case of Adrian's son Mike shows. When his father leaves, the boy feels angry, baffled and hurt. Those feelings do not go away just because the man who caused them has vanished. In fact, the reverse happens.

The only picture that Mike had of Adrian was as the man who, for some reason, abandoned him when he was two. If Adrian had seen him on a regular basis, Mike would, perhaps, have been able to build up another picture of his father. In time he might have been able to understand why Adrian felt he had to live separately from his family.

However, Mike's father was, to him, only the man who abandoned the family. Mike tried to work out why this happened. Two-year-olds are very much at the centre of their own thinking. So Mike believed that Adrian left because he, himself, was not worth staying for. This was why he constantly underachieved at school; he knew he was not worth much. Later, the adolescent Mike had another sort of problem coming to terms with his own manhood. All adolescents feel the need to rebel against the same sex parent. However, Mike's father was, to him, only the bastard who abandoned the family, nothing more. So his adolescent rebellion became extreme: he challenged substitute authority figures like teachers or policemen. This is how he got 'on the wrong side of the law'.

All these problems were not caused by Adrian's decision to live in a different house from his wife and children. They were the result of Adrian causing his son to feel wholly abandoned, and then denying the boy a chance to live through a period where father and son could, by spending time together, reach a point where Mike could understand, then forgive, the man who left their family.

There were repercussions for Adrian, too:

ADRIAN:   It was me who came off worst. After I left, the next Christmas was hell. I saw this advert with a little girl in it – same age as my daughter. I just burst out crying . . . I don't talk about my son . . . I feel this guilt about him.

Later, Adrian said something else that showed he had not made a 'clean break' at all:

ADRIAN:   For most of my life I've been what people call a womanizer. Mostly these are girls I go for, much younger than me –
ME:   How much?
ADRIAN:   Twenty years younger.
ME:   About your daughter's age?
ADRIAN:   I thought of that too. It's true – I fall in love with them. One especially – she really reminded me of my daughter, like she'd be

> now. But it was impossible, the age
> difference . . .

The term 'clean break' is a lie. It is not a break at all; the feelings for lost loved ones go on and on long after they have left the family home. Mike attacked his absent father through the policemen and teachers he confronted so aggressively. Adrian tried to reach his lost daughter through the succession of young women he loved. Nor is it clean; Mike's feelings about his father could not be resolved, and so they festered inside him, growing huge and poisonous until they could only be expressed as a murderous threat. As Adrian said of his son: 'He says if he ever met me, he'd stick a knife in me.'

Adrian's belief that the 'clean break' was best was certainly sincere. The 'clean break' doesn't work because it is based on the misguided belief that the best way to resolve emotional conflict is to keep issues simple and clear. Divorce is not at all simple. Everyone involved – husband, wife, children – is caught up in a situation that will generate powerful contradictory emotions. All the individuals involved feel conflicts with each other and within themselves. The issues are not simple and not clear. Pretending they are does not make them so. The only way out of the problem is for everyone involved to have time and peace in which to live through this difficult phase. This is true for adults, and it is true for children.

The only way your children can resolve the conflicts born of divorce is by being allowed to express and live with these contradictory emotions. They need to spend time with you to do this. The remainder of this chapter is about various ways in which you can achieve this. Before that, however, we need to consider all the obstacles that are put in the way. The biggest obstacle seems to be the law: the courts and the legal profession.

## THE LAW VERSUS THE FAMILY

ME:     When did you last see your children?

BILL:   Eight years ago. I took my daughter out for a
        birthday treat. We got back late and there was
        a row and since then I haven't seen my son or
        my daughter. We'd just gone out to celebrate.

ME:     What were the legal arrangements?

BILL:   She had custody. I had access – three hours
        every other weekend. In my mind that was the
        minimum time allowed, you see. But it was the
        maximum in her mind. I mean – there was hell
        to pay if I got them back five minutes late.

This kind of misunderstanding is common between estranged
couples. He wants to see his children as much as possible, but
she wants to begin a new life without him. In most cases it is
possible to find a compromise, but in this one, the result
was that Bill sadly lost all contact with his children:

BILL:   I tried writing to my daughter. At first there
        was no reply. Then one day I got the whole
        bundle sent back in a parcel with a note from
        her saying, 'I don't want to hear from you.'

ME:     Do you know why she did this?

BILL:   No. She's a loving girl . . . used to be anyhow.

ME:     Do you blame your wife?

BILL:   I don't really want to portion out blame. I've
        married again and I have a loving wife, and a
        son. But . . . (he sighs) I can't help thinking
        about my two. Not knowing – that's the worst.

Bill suffered the torment that all victims of the 'clean
break' undergo. He felt helpless, deeply hurt and com-

pletely baffled. He had found happiness in a new life, but his unresolved feelings for his 'two' went on and on.

The reason why Bill lost all contact with his children over a seemingly minor quarrel was because of a judge's ruling:

BILL: I just couldn't understand how this judge could sit there and say he agreed with my wife that I couldn't see my children or even talk to them on the phone.

Bill had not abandoned his family, and he kept up maintenance payments. The judge was acting 'in the best interests of the children', as he put it.

ME: Did you challenge the court's decision?
BILL: I thought about it. But I was at a low ebb – I was out of work, and I felt the cost, the financial and emotional cost, was too high. So I left it. I thought more conflict would do more harm than good.

In the course of researching this book, I heard of many cases where the legal profession and the courts made it more difficult for a divorcing couple to achieve some sort of reconciliation.

BILL: I'm amazed at the judge's lack of understanding of what it feels like to be a father. He wasn't a wise man – you expect judges to be wise. He just seemed to be intent on protecting my wife and my kids from me. But I've never harmed them. Even my wife had to admit that.

One man described a solicitor who was supposed to be a divorce expert:

'I disliked him from the start. He looked shrunken and shrivelled up. He said that he saw his job as making sure my wife didn't take me to the cleaners. I said I just wanted to make sure they had enough, but he ignored me. I meant it. Then he asked me my children's dates of birth. I told him. He said, "That's unusual, that's impressive; most men have trouble remembering!" I think he was trying to make me feel better. I never went back.'

The judge and the solicitor who specialized in divorce have two assumptions in common. Firstly, they firmly believe a divorcing couple are adversaries, locked in battle. Secondly, they assume that, as parents, fathers are emotionally less significant than mothers.

These are not isolated examples. I heard many tales of combative solicitors wrecking the communication between divorcing partners. Very few of those I interviewed had a good word to say about solicitors. From their description of events, it seems that the whole system is the problem. Husband and wife each have a solicitor whose aim is to protect their client's interests. So conflict is built into the whole procedure. Solicitors' attitudes obviously derive from the adversarial system within which they have to operate. This story shows the system at its most ridiculous:

'I don't think these solicitors are interested in reaching agreement; I think they enjoy the fight. It cannot be right that my ex-wife and I had to fight over maintenance right up to the door of the judge's chambers. As we waited in his corridor, a ridiculous little play was acted out. My ex was at one end of the corridor, I at the other; we were not allowed to talk. The two solicitors scurried back and forth between us doing a deal. That was how the maintenance was worked out, and the value of the house divided. Neither of us had time to think it out. And when it was agreed, the two solicitors shook hands and chatted on first-name terms. They ignored us.'

Clearly, the solicitors were far more interested in the combat between them than they were in their clients. This may be an exception, but I heard a lot of stories about incompetent, uncaring, lazy, even exploitative solicitors. The most common complaint was that they didn't understand what their clients were going through. This may not be because all solicitors are, as a breed, callous. It is more likely because their attitudes are formed by a system where the first concern is winning a case, and interest in conciliation between hurt, angry people comes second.

Judges were also seen as unsympathetic, unimaginative and deeply conservative when it came to the issue of custody. In the majority of cases, custody is automatically given to the mother. Indeed, to get custody, a man has to prove that his children's mother is emotionally unfit to be a parent at all. Even a mother who has abandoned her children has been known to win a custody case after turning up, years later, to reclaim them. Judges assume that a child's place is with its mother.

The well-known case of Mr Moodey is a clear example. Details of this case were sent to me by the organization Families Need Fathers. Mr Moodey divorced his wife because of her adultery. The court awarded her custody and gave Mr Moodey access.

In 1981, Mr Moodey's ex-wife and her new husband decided to emigrate with the children to South Africa. Mr Moodey objected on two grounds. Firstly, it would deny him any access, and so destroy the new relationship he had built up with his children. Secondly, he had strong objections to his children being exposed to the apartheid system.

The English Appeal Court dismissed his objections, and allowed the children to be taken to live in South Africa. The court held that Mr Moodey's objections to apartheid 'could not be taken into account' and quoted a standard precedent from 1970 in which hard Justice Sachs said: 'This court should not rightly interfere with such a reasonable way of life as is selected by that parent to whom custody has been rightly given.'

The case was taken to the European Commission on Human Rights, but they upheld the English Appeal Court ruling, and Mr Moodey's three sons now live in South Africa.

The phrase 'rightly given' betrays the assumptions made about parenthood by English courts. Despite the fact that the 1969 Divorce Reform Act removed any notion of 'blame' in divorce cases, the ruling assumes that one parent is a more fitting arbiter of how a child shall lead its first eighteen years of life. The mother is assumed to be the 'natural parent'. The father is assumed to be peripheral at best, expendable at worst. Mr Moodey's principled objection to apartheid was ignored, despite his fear of the effect on young, impressionable children. His moral principles and his parental concern were set aside. It could not have been because the divorce proved him unfit to be a parent – his wife had broken up the marriage, not him. He had paid maintenance, and had been a loving father to his children. The reason why he was less significant as a parent was because he was male.

This is, once again, a direct result of the cultural definition of 'maleness'. If people make the assumptions about the male outlined in chapter one, then of course it is difficult for them to understand that men might have something to do with the emotions associated with and required of childrearing: tenderness, gentleness, patience, tolerance of frustration, self-denial etc. Men are supposed

128

to be protectors and guiders. This perhaps explains why Frank was the *only* single father I interviewed who had won custody. However, Frank felt he was given custody for the wrong reason. The judge said that, of the two parents, Frank was showing the most concern for their education. The judge ignored the fact that Frank had, in fact, brought up his children in the home since they were babies. The same blind assumptions were at work in the case of a man who told me that he was prepared to give up his job to bring up his children. He felt that his wife was emotionally unstable, and provided the court with proof of this. The judge, however, ruled that he 'could not find sufficient reason to take this man out of work'.

This attitude that men are not natural carers is part of a much wider set of assumptions about caring and nurturing in our society. It is assumed that men should not waste their time on caring and nurturing because, really, it is women's work. Our society doesn't really value this kind of activity. For example, wages are low in caring professions like nursing and social work, or in nurturing professions like teaching, where the wages are so low that many are leaving the profession; yet what could be more important to a society than the proper education of the next generation? In financial terms, money spent on education is a good investment. The judges who pass over a father's concern for his children and the authorities that keep teachers' and nurses' wages low are acting on the assumption that to care and nurture is not as important as competing, getting and having.

It is no wonder, then, that I met so many fathers who felt beleaguered because their role as as parent was not recognized as the divorce proceeded.

It is important to assert and claim your right as a father when going through legal proceedings. The best way to achieve this is to insist on joint custody of the children, rather than allow the mother sole custody, leaving you with merely a limited period of access. Many of the men whose access had been whittled away did not have joint custody. When their parental involvement became marginal, most of them complained that the legal profession took little or no interest in their feelings that they wanted to maintain a relationship with the children they loved.

## WHY FATHERS NEED ACCESS TO THEIR CHILDREN

Fatherhood can bring out a side of a man's nature that otherwise often gets little chance of expression.

'Babies, children, they need you because they're so helpless. At first you *have* to love them. I mean, I'd never been needed like that, so I was amazed at her and how I felt. Then you love them because you love them. I love her because she's herself, I suppose.'

'People who never have kids don't know what they're missing. I watched them grow, and all their achievements, like walking. I was so *proud*. Proud in a way you can't be proud about anything else.'

'When you love a child you feel bigger. I don't mean macho. It's more generous. It does you good. And you have this emotional link into the future.'

'At first I thought living alone, without my kids, would be restful. But it isn't, because I don't belong anywhere now, except when I'm with them. When they're at my house, it's a home and I love the noise and mess. When they go the house dies.'

The last comment shows particularly well how fathers need their children just as much as children need their fathers. It is important to assert this need, because it is often invisible to those who are held to be 'experts' in law and divorce. They work in a system based on competition. They need to be reminded of what must be *saved* in a divorce. Ideally, a man's relationship with his children is life-enhancing for parent and child. It is important to preserve and protect what is life-enhancing. The best way to do this is to insist on humane access arrangements. Joint custody, rather than simple 'access', establishes your right to be considered as a parent of equal influence. You need to create the circumstances in which you and your child or children can restore your former intimacy and build up a relationship for the future. This means spending time together.

## WHY CHILDREN NEED ACCESS TO THEIR FATHERS

When a father leaves home, a child is naturally distressed. This distress may not show immediately. Reactions will vary a lot depending on age, sex and their place in the family. However calmly a child takes the separation, it is certain that some of the following reactions will take place:

A child may become depressed. Persistent depression shows up in failure to thrive, failure to learn and failure to care for themselves.

Children will rationalize the loss of an important person by inventing in their minds a reason why the lost person is no longer interested in them. In many cases they decide it is because they have been bad or that they're unlovable. This leads to loss of self-esteem.

Children may split their ambiguous feelings about their father. They may convert their positive memories of a lost father into a fantasy that is far removed from the person they knew. This fantasy-person may become idealized and be felt to be someone who will meet the child's every need whilst making no demands in return. Alongside this, the child may be storing up anger, hatred and resentment. This will show up in big tantrums, an increase in aggression directed at others who, to the child, stand for the father.

Children may play emotional games with their separated parents. Sometimes they will try to play one parent off against the other; a typical issue is pocket money. Sometimes they'll try to bring the parents back together. This can reach quite dangerous levels: some children are so desperate that they have serious accidents. They know that the anxiety will bring the parents together at their hospital bedside.

The answer to all these reactions is that a child needs the regular presence of the parent who has left. The child's ambiguous, tempestuous emotions need to be tested against the reality of the father's personality. A child that is depressed needs the reassuring love and attention of its father if it is to recover. A child that believes it is responsible for the father leaving needs his reassurance and continued attention if it is to get over the feeling of guilt.

If a child splits its love for its father off from its anger at his leaving, then it is even more vital to have regular access. Only prolonged contact with the father will sustain the memory of the father's real personality, and counteract the dangerous idealization. A safe relationship with its father will allow the child to express its anger: both father and child need to live through this period in order to reach an understanding. The child can only love its father realistically after it has forgiven him for leaving. It can forgive more easily if it understands why he left. This understanding will come sometimes only after years. Often a child needs to grow into adolescence before it really understands why male–female relationships can break down.

Children would much rather love their parents than hate

them. By securing reasonable humane access, you are helping the child to love both parents and so build a positive attitude to life. In short, access is a child's right, and a parent's duty.

Access should be planned to start as soon as the parents separate. If the husband–wife relationship is still acrimonious, then it is best to seek the help of neutral figures. They can be professionals or friends and relatives. How access is arranged depends on the age and maturity of the child. This rough guide to the needs of a child at different ages is based on the work of Melanie Klein, John Bowlby and Bruno Bettleheim – all leading experts in child psychology.

*Ages 1–3*
In these early years, a child is extremely attached to its mother, especially if she is the person who has more contact with it. That attachment should dictate who has main care of the child.

The other parent's access should be frequent and brief; perhaps several evenings a week at bathtime. The visit should not be such that it takes the child away from the mother (or attached parent) for too long. A child of this age could not cope with an all-day outing.

*Pre-school children, age 3–5*
Children of this age have a limited sense of time. It will understand, 'I'll see you tomorrow', but 'I'll see you next week' will probably have little meaning. A gap of a week will feel like months to a child of this age. More mature children of this age group can cope with a night away from mother. Visits to the child should be more often than once a week.

*School-age children, age 5–12*
At five or six, children develop a more sophisticated sense of time. At this stage, once-weekly access may

be enough to maintain a worthwhile relationship. Ideally, the meetings should be more often than this. What is vital, though, is that the access should be regular. If access is every Saturday, then it must be *every* Saturday. A child will get a sense of security from the feeling that the week has a structure to it and that father's visit is part of that structure. Children will become distressed if a father seems to be unreliable about access or if the mother prevents him from seeing the child at a regular time. If it is necessary to alter an access arrangement, the father should explain why to both the parent *and* the child, before making another arrangement to visit or see the child.

By this age, a child will be able to stay away from mother for longer periods, because the need for attachment will be less intense.

Children of this age are also forming new attachments – to friends and a community via the school. This needs to be respected and encouraged by the father. He needs to make room for his child's friends, too. Above all, a child should not feel that there is any competition for time between father and friends.

### Adolescents
As children develop through puberty, it will become possible to arrange access direct with the adolescent. They must, however, be encouraged to take the responsibility of informing the parent with whom they live.

I've used 'access' to cover visits, outings, the child staying at the father's flat or house, and holidays. Each couple will differ over what 'access' means in terms of time and place.

These are a child's basic needs when its parents divorce. However, there are many cases where a child does not get even these, and access is prevented. The most common cause of this is when children become a pawn in a game of emotional conflict played out between the warring couple.

## USING CHILDREN AS A WEAPON

The saddest man I met was Tony. He is homosexual and a Christian. He had married because he felt that it was his duty to do so. He had great affection for his wife, and even more for his daughter Faith. However, after several years, the marriage began to fall apart. Then one night he told his wife about his homosexuality:

TONY: It was so hard to tell her. But I never expected the reaction I got. She reacted like I was a monster. She ordered me out of the house then and there. She wouldn't even let me say goodbye to Faith.

From then on, Tony had to face a continual barrage of abuse, and did not see his daughter for a year.

TONY: The court gave me access. But my wife was so bitter she made them order me not to take her to my new home. I could take her out, but never home. In case me and my gay friends corrupted her.

ME: The court agreed with her?

TONY: Yup. I see her once a month. We go out, but I can't have any kind of life with her.

ME: How do you feel about that?

TONY: I can't tell you, friend. I could write a book about it. I keep her photo near me all the time. And this letter.

135

Faith had written Tony a letter in which she said she did not believe he was an evil man, and that she loved him:

TONY:   My wife's been poisoning her against me. But I've got this letter . . .

This is only one example of a child's mother trying to influence it against the father who has left. In most cases, it happens because the unhappy relationship between the parents has not been resolved. In this case, Faith's mother was using her as a weapon to hurt Tony. No doubt she thought consciously that she was protecting the girl, but her action was deeply damaging to the child.

Unfortunately, I found many, many cases where adults were unable to contain their feelings at the end of a marriage, and started to use access to the children as a weapon.


## USING ACCESS AS A WEAPON

When Chris married Julia he did so because he found her very attractive and lovable. There was, he said, something childlike about her. She looked on him as a sort of protector. He arrived in her life just as she had finished a relationship with a violent man who abused her a lot. Chris married Julia, and they seemed to be happy and secure.

All was well for a few years. Then she began to have brief affairs. After admitting these, Julia was very contrite. She was 'extra sweet', and 'very adoring' of Chris in the months that followed these 'little lapses' (his description). Then it all happened again.

They separated, but after a week she wanted him back desperately. Soon after getting back together, Julia was pregnant. She was a most adoring mother. However, she behaved as if the baby was entirely hers. She lost interest in anything other than the baby. Chris found himself 'a stranger in my own house'. Still, he carried on being forgiving, tolerant and understanding.

CHRIS: I realized she needed to get something out of her system, you see.
ME: What?
CHRIS: Oh, it was all to do with her childhood.
ME: But you said she was making you very unhappy, 'undermining' you –
CHRIS: Yes, but she couldn't help it.
ME: But she was an adult woman, able to have children, so surely –
CHRIS: You don't understand. She couldn't help it. I know I was a fool. I know!

One day Chris came home to find the whole house stripped of furniture, pictures, ornaments, books etc. His wife had disappeared with the child. After a month, Chris found her. She was living a hundred miles away. She wouldn't speak to him or see him; nor would she let him see the baby. She wanted him out of her life, *now*. He sued for divorce, citing her adultery, and applying for access to visit his son:

CHRIS: It was a nightmare what happened. The court gave me access, but she'd always have a reason for my not seeing him. I'd travel all that way, and find a note on the door, saying they'd gone out. I made applications to the court, and they warned her. Then she fooled the doctor into giving her sick notes for them, so I'd arrive and find this doctor's note on the door; a different illness each week.

Eventually, Chris got access, but only after the court threatened Julia with prison.

ME:     Now you have access, is it helping build a good relationship with your son?

CHRIS:  I don't know. At first he wouldn't go with me because he didn't know who I was. Then, after a while, we got into this pattern: he'd arrive on Friday night and within hours he'd have a tantrum, smash something, refuse to eat . . . lots of different kinds of angry outbursts. I'd have to be strict. After that, it was OK. But he sort of had to go crazy first.

It is obvious that the instability of Chris and Julia's marriage, followed by a period of stress and disruption surrounding the access issue, had made their son very anxious indeed. He had to test how far he could go with his father before he could feel safe. If Chris and Julia had been able to negotiate reasonable access terms, that disturbance in his life would have been minimized. The boy would have felt sad, baffled and angry because his parents had parted. But he would not have been so deeply terrified. This terror arose from the bitter war about access between his parents.

The reason they fought, at a distance, over the issue of their son, was because Chris and Julia found it impossible to resolve their differences face to face. At no point in the marriage did Julia confront the reasons why she felt compelled to be constantly unfaithful. At no point in the marriage did Chris confront Julia with how hurt and angry he was. Instead, she tried to make herself behave like a good girl, and he tried to be totally understanding. Both of them spent a lot of time denying what they were really feeling. These emotions had to come out somehow. Julia was constantly trying to make Chris feel excluded. First she did this by having affairs, then she did it by becoming totally wrapped up in caring for their son. She used other males to express her feelings.

Chris had a responsibility in this situation: a responsibility to speak out and say that Julia had no right to treat him this way, no right to misuse their son, and no right to prevent the son having contact with his father. However, Chris did not speak out.

One vital issue was ignored by the couple:

ME:     Did you ask her if the child was yours?
CHRIS:  Oh, that went through my mind. All the
        time. But I never put it to her in so many
        words. I'll never know, I suppose . . .

Julia's behaviour, getting Chris to come a hundred miles and then locking him out, was simply a continuation of her former tactics. The only difference was that both of them had stored up so much violent emotion that communication had become impossible. The only way Chris could act was through a lawyer and a judge. Only then did Julia back down, grudgingly and fearfully. In such an atmosphere, sensible discussion is impossible.

Neither Chris nor Julia took any responsibility for their emotions. Julia felt so guilty she had to run away. Chris couldn't express his deep fear, anger and distress about the child. So when they had any contact at all, every subject was supercharged with unresolved emotions both had tried to avoid. When they came to negotiate access, all that came out was anger, distress, fear, guilt and all the rest. Instead of protecting their son from these emotions, they filled him up with it all.

Few people set out to use their children as pawns in a deadly emotional game, but this is exactly what happens if adults refuse to take responsibility for their feelings and actions. A quarrel between parents should remain between parents.

## THE SUCCESSFUL ACCESS RELATIONSHIP

Access can work well to produce a lasting healthy relationship.

STEPHEN: It has worked out. When we were together the quarrels between my wife and myself were acrimonious. I think we both realized this couldn't go on; it was beginning to affect the children.

ME: Did you try to protect them?

STEPHEN: Oh yes, but if you're in a house, all together, there's an atmosphere isn't there? Now some people stay together for the kids. What I say is we separated for the kids. But I'd seen so many of our friends make a dog's dinner of it, so I said to my wife, 'We're going to do this properly.'

Stephen's attitude was one of firmness, but kindness. He discussed several options with his wife.

STEPHEN: We went through the possibilities.

ME: Custody. Joint custody. Access?

STEPHEN: Oh yes, but much more important when and how we split up. When I'd see the kids, how long for. Everything – we discussed it all. Then we did it and explained everything to them. My wife was so good – she insisted that it wasn't

anyone's fault, and not theirs and they'd
see me a lot. It was amazing because it was
my fault in a way; I'd had the affair, not
her. She's a very strong woman; I liked her
more than I had for years.

It is interesting that, in trying to act in the best interests of their children, Stephen and his wife moved towards greater mutual understanding.

ME:      What were the problems?
STEPHEN: There was a period when my daughter got
         very distressed about leaving me each
         Sunday.

Children do tend to go through a period of disturbances when an access arrangement is newly in place. Repeated minor illnesses are common, as well as sleeping problems, allergies, headaches and so on. These are emotionally useful, because the child often needs to be looked after in a way that is appropriate to a baby. It is the child's way of reminding the adult that it needs greater care and attention over this period: regression of a sort is quite normal for a while. It's important to take these illnesses seriously and not let the child feel it's not real. Asthma, for example, is a very real experience, and it's a common allergic reaction. The child should be given love, care and attention, but should not be allowed to manipulate the parents into altering access arrangements.

STEPHEN: Good things came out of our access
         arrangement eventually. My wife and I
         stopped getting at each other because we
         had to make sure our son and daughter
         were OK. And their relationship became
         very strong, very strong indeed.

This is the point I want to end on. Access need not be a pathetic substitute for what existed before the marriage break-up. It is possible to create new, strong, realistic relationships with (and between) your children. To do it, you have to be strong. You have to take responsibility for your part in the failure of the marriage. You have to endure a period of emotional upheaval when everyone's feelings will be ambiguous and perhaps violent. The point of doing this is that you give everyone a chance to preserve something that is good and life-enhancing: the happiness of your children, and maybe, through that, a more realistic kind of relationship with your ex-wife.

# CHAPTER SEVEN

# Money, Property and Assets

'Ah, so you're writing a book about the emotional aspects of divorce; so it isn't about the practicalities then . . .'

This became a familiar reaction as I did my research and interviews for this book. Both men and women assumed that issues of money and property were practical issues, not emotional issues, and were best left to legal experts.

This view is mistaken on two counts. First, money and property are highly emotive issues; second, at least seventy-five per cent of my interviewees claimed their solicitors were incompetent, uncaring or lazy, and that judges' decisions were arbitrary and unjust.

Andy's case is not untypical of what I heard. He wrote to me:

'In 1981, my wife took to herself a lover, who, like herself, worked with social services, and they were in close proximity each and every day. This love romance happened within the walls of a hostel for mentally handicapped persons, which was an ideal place to hide their affair, and to start to work towards milking me, the family, and to go into massive debts, mainly for him. He managed to get a new car out of her, furnishings for his flat, where she had his key, and also spent nights there, pretending to be on night work for the handicapped.'

When his wife left him and the children he found that
'. . . their relationship had taken hundreds of pounds from
the home, banks, loan companies and the like.'

As if this was not bad enough, he found himself and his
children badly treated by two sets of solicitors and a judge:

'I went to a team of solicitors, three days after she left
home, to start divorce proceedings against her and her
lover. And this is now the time that things really got
"screwed up" by the so-called legal profession. I was
told by a solicitor that I could not sue for divorce, even
though I had laid before him the whole merits of the
case. I showed him bank letters about bounced
cheques, money being obtained by false pretences,
loan company applications showing the way in which
they obtained money quoting items for our home, and
letters of "love" found from both of them, endearing
terms which, if read, could not lead to any other
conclusion about their motives. All this evidence and
not a reason? I was told it was too early to worry about
divorce action, and that they had to try reconciliation
first. I said that I would not have her back, and that
she would never want to come back. But these
solicitors say they know the business, so I left it to
them.

'After more than a month of pussy-footing around,
back came the reply, NO. Then, horror upon horror,
they still did not pursue the divorce. Then they said
that they would go for custodial proceedings instead.
I already had custody, down to the fact that my ex-
wife had written a letter saying that she did not want
the children any more, and that I should have the
custody and a natural right. But, this was not enough
for the solicitor to proceed for divorce. In the end, my
ex-wife decided to sue me instead, quoting fictitious

happenings, which could have been refuted in any court hearing by my elder children, neighbours, relatives and friends. Since then, not one solicitor has done anything to present my case. Not one item of evidence has ever been used to bring the truth to the light. In fact, I was now termed the 'respondent', the GUILTY party. No one wanted to represent me in taking the matter to court to justify my claims, to prove debts, money frauds, and the like.

'I changed solicitors, but that did not do me much good anyway. I had to wait for her to get settlement proceedings into court. Again, no one, but no one, had any time to present my case, and upon that fateful afternoon in court during settlement, I was supposed to be represented by a barrister. What a laugh. I spent five minutes with him before the hearing. With all the evidence in front of him, including her later convictions for theft and burglary with others, I did not stand a chance.

'The hearing was spent mainly arguing about the price of our home, and what it should fetch on the market. She wanted me evicted to get her share. This I had to stand up and shout about, because I could see that no one was really interested about myself and the children. I did manage to get a word in about this, and the judge, being in a pretty sour mood, did say that I could live there with the children providing that 1) *I did not marry again*, that *I did not co-habitate with any female*, or *have any female live in with us, even in a care situation*; 2) *I must not sell the property, or let or lease, or have lodgers; failing any of these articles, I would have to pay her, immediately, half the value*. This really hits at the kids, for without them, I would not have any need to fight for the home. To state that I must not marry without forfeiting the home is an *infringement upon*

145

*human rights, denying the children* ever knowing a mother's love in the home. Many a time, in the last few years, I have met some lovely ladies, I could have got to know them a lot better. But constantly with the thought of our home *being lost* if I did pursue friendship to such a point that I may fall in love again, I usually push them away, and feel very much sorrow.'

Andy's rage and bitterness are evident all through his letter. So, too, is a sense of impotence. However, it is worth asking why he had to end up so devastated. Was it avoidable? Could he have *insisted* that his solicitor start divorce proceedings against his wife? Could he have found a better solicitor? Could he have appealed against this judgement?

The answer to all these questions is yes: the client does instruct his solicitor, not vice versa. There are, somewhere in England, solicitors who are trustworthy and efficient. Finally, the principle of appeal is built into British justice. So, why did Andy end this letter to me saying:

'Let me summarise with these points:
1) I must not marry again or have any live-in female companion, even for the children's sake.
2) I cannot appeal against any court decision, now or ever.
3) I am being made to pay for adultery, the debts of two lovers, and being treated like the guilty party, all because of corrupt solicitors allowing me to be placed as 'respondent'.
4) Not one scrap of the mass of evidence was ever used to bring the truth to open court. A sure indictment of the way solicitors treat innocent families.'

I felt sorry for Andy, but I do think he could have had more control over the situation than he thought. He did not need to be the victim of what seems to be a bunch of malicious, jealous, exploitative people. It is worth asking why he felt this way and trying to discover what prevented him from seeking and achieving a more positive outcome.

## MONEY EQUALS LOVE

When a loved one dies, those who survive will be very anxious over what has been left for them in the will. It may seem that they are being mercenary, but in fact they are anxious about how important they were to the deceased. If you are left a lot of money it is a sign that you were important to the loved one. If you were left less than other people, it is a sign you were less significant. Put crudely, the amount of money given is felt to equal the amount of love felt.

When there are arguments over a will it is possible for some beneficiaries to imagine the others are stealing from them, or that there are secret funds not available to them. Everyone is taken over by feelings about what is owed to them. In fact, the money is a gift, not a right. All this is complicated enough when someone dies. It's even more of a minefield when property is divided up after love has died but the people are living on.

In Andy's case he felt his love was murdered by his wife and her lover. He felt overpoweringly jealous, and hated his wife. He felt she and her new lover were malicious and exploiting him. Meanwhile he felt impotent and had to take their affair full in the face.

When Andy discovered his wife's affair, he was so choked up with emotion that he could not communicate with her. It sounds as if, at that early stage, his wife felt so guilty that she just wanted to get out quickly. At that point, I suspect Andy could have had any settlement he wanted. However, he had not been able to express direct to his wife all his feelings about how she had betrayed his love and humiliated him. Because he could not express all this, nothing could be resolved between them.

As a consequence, what happened afterwards was super-charged with those feelings of jealousy, betrayal, impotence and the malice of others. It became impossible for the couple to put the past behind them and negotiate a fair share-out of the money and property. Money and property was the language they were using to continue their unresolved relationship. Andy felt that all that his marriage had brought to his life had been stolen and given to his wife's lover. Everyone around him was felt to be uncaring, even hostile. The final settlement was obviously ridiculous, but Andy felt he must put up with it. Andy was so caught up with feelings about others' injustice to him that he found it almost impossible to see any alternative way of going on. His wife's betrayal affected all his thinking. His sense of his own impotence smothered his will to have this wrong put right. He could not impose his will on his solicitor, and so was led by him. Andy did not allow for the possibility that he could find a solicitor who was honest and able; but such people do exist. He could not bring himself to use the principle of appeal that is built into English law.

Most unfortunate of all, his jealousy was so overwhelm-ing that it felt to him as if everyone was preventing him from loving someone other than his wife. This happened because Andy was unable to express his powerful feel-ings of jealousy and hate to his wife direct. Perhaps he was so full of volcanic emotion that he was afraid of what might happen. He had good reason; after all, people murder because of jealousy. However, his emotions demanded to come out somehow, and he felt it as an outside force attacking him through the lawyers and judges he had to deal with.

Andy did have legitimate grievances and it would be quite wrong to suggest that he had somehow brought his troubles on himself. However, he did have more options than he believed.

To sort out matters of property and money you do need a clear idea of the issues and principles behind the share-out. You need to make your judgement in as fair a way as possible, especially when children are concerned. The problem for divorcing couples is that they are called on to act in this Olympian way when they may be full of hate, grief, a sense of betrayal and desire for revenge. Once they have separated, the danger is that they use the issues of money, property and (as we have seen) children to say all the things that they could not say direct.

## LOST LOVE AND THE DESIRE FOR POWER

In divorce, generally, the more people feel unable to express their feelings the more vindictive they can be when it comes to sharing out property and assets.

When he married her, Paul's wife seemed to be a gentle, kind but slightly anxious woman; he loved her:

PAUL: I fell head over heels in love with Mary. I rejoiced in her body. I loved our lovemaking and wrote poems to her. She had a Presbyterian background and felt guilty about pre-marital sex, but even after we married, I don't think she enjoyed it. But we loved each other very much.

149

Paul was loving and kind. They had a lovely house, and he provided for her and their growing family. He encouraged Mary to work and was concerned she was happy and fulfilled.

How, then, when it came to divorce, did Mary end up blackmailing Paul, threatening him with public exposure if she did not get the children, the house (with no mortgage), and a new car every two years, and an income of £500 per month?

One reason may be that Paul had a one-night stand. However, he loved Mary, and their relationship was sexually active all the time. Paul decided to confess this one lapse, and promised never to repeat it. Mary's reaction was, at first, one of relief:

PAUL:  She had been frightened by my grey pallor, silence and fearful eyes. Her initial reaction when I told her was 'Is that all?' But then, over the next nine years, the full implications revealed themselves to us both.

The reason why this one lapse became so important was because Paul had had sex with another man. Over those nine years, he never stopped loving Mary, but he could not ignore the fact that his strongest sexual feelings were for men.

When they did split up, Mary's real feelings came out. Her rather puritanical background made even heterosexual intimacy a possible source of anxiety. When she discovered that the man who shared her bed was homosexual, then she probably felt violent disgust and extreme hostility. This was, initially, so great that she could not express it. She just said 'Is that all?' But, underneath, her feelings were growing more and more violent.

So, when it came to dividing up the joint property, Mary's revengeful feelings took over.

PAUL: She said if I didn't give her what she wanted, then she'd tell all our friends, the whole village, everyone, that I was a 'poof', as she called it.

This seems a violent change of character. In fact, like Andy, Mary's desire for revenge came from a feeling of powerlessness. For a woman it is bad enough to have a female rival; but it is possible to compete with the other woman. However, a wife cannot hope to win her husband's love back if her rival is a man. She cannot compete at all.

If her feeling of powerlessness is added to her disgust and hostility, then it is no wonder Mary acted so vindictively. At least by blackmailing her husband she could have back some of the power she felt she had lost to the other man.

Mary felt she had lost out entirely in the area of love and intimacy. She made up for this by seeking to get as much power as she could in other areas. That would make her feel safe and less liable to be hurt in the future. She got that power over her husband by blackmailing him, and ensured she'd keep the power by taking as much as she could out of the marriage, regardless of who had put what into the relationship. Mary would probably have preferred to have had all of Paul through love; since she couldn't have that, she had all of him through power.

Paul was devastated by this change in his wife. He felt guilty, but also felt that she was reacting in a wild and reckless way. He gave her what she wanted, but the bitterness remained between them. Paul was impressive: he said he had tried to understand her and still felt love for her. He was missing his children deeply.

In both Andy's and Paul's cases, the couples found it

impossible to deal with the emotional upheaval in their lives. What is needed in such cases is a neutral conciliator whose aim is to help the couple resolve their differences and part with good grace. If a husband and wife can communicate enough to seek such help, then the couple's need for a safe, peaceful haven in which to express and resolve their feelings can be met. What usually happens, however, is that each of them goes to a solicitor. This is someone whose first interest is not conciliation, but doing their best for a client. A solicitor is not, by definition, a neutral conciliator. Maybe the men who expect their solicitors to be caring actually need another kind of professional help at the time.

At the end of this book, I have included a list of contact numbers through which you can get a consultation with various kinds of conciliation services.


## MONEY, VALUE AND SELF-ESTEEM

Nicholas said of himself, 'I'm always described as a perfect gentleman. I am, I suppose.' His father had created a jewellery business and, in time, Nicholas inherited it. At first, it flourished. He married in his forties; his wife was Danish and some twenty years younger. Then they divorced:

NICHOLAS: I was, you see, obliged to leave my home. Nowhere to go, either. I'd got no funds. My wife was in charge of the financial aspect. I'd made her a managing director of the firm.

ME: Why?

NICHOLAS: Well I was training her, you see, to inherit the company. Now, she was spirited. She said she couldn't run it my

way, my father's way. She had to run it
*her* way. Of course, I understood,
supported her. But, well . . .

ME:        It didn't work out?

NICHOLAS:    Something of a disaster. Oh dear me,
yes . . .

Nicholas laughed, at this point, and shrugged almost
apologetically.

ME:        Did you try to stop this disaster?

NICHOLAS:    I saw it coming, but would she listen to
me? No. (*He grins*) In return for making
her Managing Director I was to be more
involved with the home and children.
Behind my back she was having an affair
with my partner. But I only found that
out later, mind.

ME:        Why do you think she behaved this way?

NICHOLAS:    I found, to my regret, that everything
had been a deliberate move by my wife
to obtain control over the family's
property.

ME:        Did she get that control?

NICHOLAS:    Well, yes she did. I ended up bankrupt,
you see.

Nicholas seemed to have co-operated in the process that
led to his bankruptcy:

NICHOLAS:    Yes, I also made the mistake of passing
on to her the shares belonging to my
father at his death.

Obviously, this goes beyond the bounds of mere financial
mismanagement. Why did Nicholas invite such disaster?

The roots of this can be found in Nicholas's rather low self-esteem. All through the interview he had a self-deprecatory air. He had plainly been exploited, betrayed and deceived; yet he spent a lot of time apologizing for his conduct. He described those who wronged him in a very mild way:

ME:          What was your wife like?
NICHOLAS:    Oh, a bit cold. But that's Danes for you.
             It's something in their culture.
ME:          And your father?
NICHOLAS:    Somewhat distant character, he was.
             Always busy; so he had a lot else on his
             mind. Than me . . . I mean. Mmm.

His father treated Nicholas like a child, keeping him away from the family business and short of money. Nicholas did not rebel that much, but tried to occupy his time by travelling; he joined the army for a while.
Nicholas's father was giving him clear signals that he was not much value as a son, and not suited to shouldering responsibility. The trouble was that Nicholas believed this, and so came to share his father's low opinion of him. This is why he complained so mildly about being cheated of his livelihood: part of him agreed that this was the sort of thing that ought to happen to someone like him.

To use a term coined in chapter five, Nicholas's Internal Parent was saying to him something like this: 'You can't handle this business. This is something for adults like me. Entrust it to someone like me, who has a cold eye; a businessman.' This kind of voice inside your head gives you a low opinion of your ability to cope; in other words, you have low self-esteem.

The problem with having low esteem is that it is a vicious circle. To break out, you need to feel outraged that

154

someone treats you so badly. To feel outraged you have to have an idea of what it means to be treated well. Furthermore, you need to feel that you deserve to be treated well. That comes from experiencing the wellbeing created by being treated well. Nicholas's experience was the opposite; he was used to being discounted and treated with disdain. He was drawn to a wife who was like his father: cold, distant and disapproving:

NICHOLAS:   Funny, but before she'd marry me she
                 insisted I have a medical check.
ME:   Why?
NICHOLAS:   To make sure I could give her children. I
                 thought that sensible. It's the law in
                 Denmark, I think.

Once again, Nicholas went along with someone he needed making him prove that he was worth the trouble of loving. He had found someone who spoke with the voice of his Internal Parent. His wife's condition may have been valid in Denmark, but they married in England.

ME:   Wasn't she marrying you for yourself?
NICHOLAS:   Yes, but I think she wanted to make sure.

If you feel you are of low value, then it makes it difficult to believe that you have the right to own assets of any value. Nicholas's father retained full control over the family business right up to the day he died. Within a few years of taking over, Nicholas was busy passing control of it over to his new young wife; who, as we have seen, was a similar character type to his father. This was not because Nicholas had in any way failed at running the family business. On the contrary, I got the impression he was doing rather well, and managing it prudently:

155

ME:        Did the business run into problems when
           you took over?
NICHOLAS:  No, not really. Well, I had to decide
           whether to open another branch. I
           decided to wait and see for a year or so,
           and then things looked good, so we went
           ahead.

This action of handing over a valuable asset had nothing
to do with his business performance. It had everything to
do with the way Nicholas felt about his own value, or lack
of value, as a human being.

Our feelings about assets like money and property are
rooted in our personal beliefs about value. If a child grows
up feeling it is valued for itself, then he or she has less of a
problem sorting out what is owed to others, and what is
owed to the self. Nicholas believed he was of little value,
and so was convinced there were others who should have
what was valuable. He was simply giving back the assets
that, at some deep level, he felt he did not deserve. His wife
was, to him, far more valuable than Nicholas himself, so
he gave her all that was of value. Of course, he regretted
and resented this, but too late. His behaviour may seem
foolish and totally unnecessary, but it does obey a kind of
deadly logic.

## MONEY SPEAKS LOUDER THAN WORDS

Could Nicholas have seen that his wife was up to no good?
Could he have halted the chain of events that led to her
taking all the assets? The answer is, I think, that he could
have read the signs, and could have acted. But it would have
required that he felt he had the right to speak out and the
right to intervene. He may well have known rationally

156

what had to be done, but did not feel he had been given the resources to do what he knew needed to be done. This, in fact, is the definition of low self-esteem: feeling unable to deal with life because you have inadequate resources within you.

The problem with divorce is that both partners will, at some point, have exactly that feeling. If their opinion of their own value is dented, this will distort how they feel about the assets from the marriage that have monetary value. The issues of income, expenditure and assets become a language with which to express pent up emotions.

SIMON: My wife and I split up after I'd had an affair. I stopped the affair and I felt very guilty about it all, and I really tried to make the marriage work. I really tried. But it wasn't going to work. I thought we'd decided on an amicable break up, mainly for the children.

However, his wife began to demand enormous sums for maintenance.

SIMON: She knew I couldn't pay; she *knew*. She wouldn't even try to find work for herself and so I had to work all hours to pay her. She could have worked; the kids were fifteen and eighteen.

After a while, Simon protested that he could not make enough money to pay this level of maintenance.

SIMON: Then her solicitor demanded I fill in a statement of income and swear it in court or something. It was ridiculous. I'd done the same job for fifteen years and she knew what

I earned. She told the solicitor to get me to
swear I didn't have a secret account
somewhere! I thought she was going mad. I
was really worried about her.

Simon's wife was behaving this way because she felt that
when he had left her, he had taken all that was valuable to
her. Her perception of how much Simon possessed was
distorted by the feeling that he had deprived her of
something that had been cherished. She was using the
language of assets and money to say, 'You took all that was
valuable in my life, and I want it back.' She felt she had no
assets, and he had too many. That conviction distorted her
view of Simon's real income. The fact that she did not feel
able even to look for a job herself could be put down to a
feeling that she was so lacking in value that no one would
want to employ her. There was, in her mind, a direct
connection between her feelings of emptiness inside and the
size of her husband's income. Again, it may seem she was
acting oddly, but there was a logic to it.

On a practical level, divorce always leaves both partners
a lot poorer. Both of them will experience a drop in income;
a change of lifestyle may be imposed on them. That, too,
will alter the way they perceive money and assets.

PETE: For years I would wake up at five in the
morning in a cold sweat, worrying about
money and maintenance. Even when there was
enough to pay her, I'd worry would there be
enough next month?

ME: Did you resent paying her so much?

PETE: I'd like to say I didn't, but, yes, I did resent it.
I felt she was wasting it, what I'd earned. And
when she got a new boy-friend I *really* resented
paying her. I mean, I knew it mostly went on

the kids, and I couldn't begrudge that,
obviously. But she'd thrown me out and I had
to pay her . . . it sticks in your throat –

ME:       *And* pay for her boy-friend?

PETE:   And her fucking boy-friend . . . yeah! I knew
it went on the kids, though . . .

Pete's own account shows how his bitterness and jealousy distorted his view of how his wife spent money. It was all part of his picture of her as someone irresponsible and fickle, and this affected how he felt she dealt with money. He knew this wasn't the whole story, but he had to struggle to maintain a more realistic view of the situation.

For both these couples, there were real problems of making one income stretch to cover two households. It is very difficult to retain a realistic view of each other's income, expenditure and assets when the division of valuables is used as a way of expressing a deep, inner sense of deprivation.

However, if a couple does face up to the real issues, then it becomes possible to achieve what both partners need: a sensible, responsible provision for the future. If two adults have loved each other and can express, somehow, that they still care about each other, then it need not be impossible for an ex-husband to acknowledge that he should help support his ex-wife and children, or for his ex-wife to have a realistic idea of what her former partner can afford.

It is important that the couple work out these issues themselves. Otherwise decisions will be made at a distance by solicitors and judges. There are people in the legal profession who genuinely do want to help a divorcing couple. But if these professionals are put in the position of making decisions about money, property and assets, then one of the couple is bound to feel a settlement has been imposed on them. If the couple make the decisions, using solicitors for advice, then the danger of a serious rift is diminished.

Of course, each case is different. But divorcing couples should try to deal with emotional issues separately from the division of assets. Once the couple have faced their emotional differences, it *is* possible to divide money and property in such a way that each partner can have the best possible start to their new life.

# CHAPTER EIGHT

# The Road to Recovery: Strategies, Pitfalls, Options

Much of this book has focused on the mourning process that takes place during and after divorce. We have examined the ways in which divorcees tend to block this process, and seen the consequences of doing so: the 'precise psychological task' Freud speaks of remains incomplete; the divorcee fails to 'detach his memories and hopes from the lost person'.

This final chapter is about ways in which we can create the conditions that will help the process of healthy mourning, so that it becomes possible to build a new life.

## THE PRIMARY NEED: A HAVEN

When you have to leave your wife and family it is vital that you do not walk out of that front door into a no-man's-land that lacks friendly support. You need a place to go where you can be yourself.

'Where to go?' is a pressing problem for a man when a couple separates. At first it can be comforting to return to your parents' house. Staying with friends is an attractive possibility. A man who has had an affair whilst he was married may simply move in with his girl-friend. This can be the most attractive alternative of all, because it will feel like the separation is really the start of a new life.

However, if you have been through the trauma of all that goes into ending a marriage you will need, above all, a place where you will not feel inhibited about feeling and expressing all the strong, contradictory emotions that are an inevitable part of the mourning process. If you choose to live with other people, you should consider how they will be affected by the changes that will take place in you. If they are likely not to like it, then you may find that you'll be inhibited by their constant presence. You may then feel it is better for you to live alone for a period.

Going to live with family, friends or girl-friends may be problematic and it's as well to know this.

## THE REACTIONS OF YOUR FAMILY

Your family may feel very ambiguous about your divorce. For example, your parents may feel rather guilty as well as concerned. They may be asking themselves, 'What did we do wrong? Did we fail him as parents?' One man I spoke to left his wife and went to live with his parents. They were so upset and remorseful that he spent much of the time comforting them when he himself was greatly in need of love and reassurance.

Your family may be very concerned to sort out whose fault it was that your marriage did not work out. As we saw in chapter three, it can be unhealthy to get stuck in a phase where blame is the main concern. Your family may feel better if they can blame someone, whether it's your ex-wife or you, because this will assuage any guilt they may be feeling.

If you have brothers or sisters they may take sides in a different way. Divorce can resurrect old rivalries. A sister may resent her brother's wife and so blame her when the marriage ends. A married brother may feel that his sister's husband has been irresponsible. There are many other possible scenarios. Even when your family is taking your side the effect can feel pressurizing. Alternatively, if they disapproved of the marriage, there may be an undercurrent of 'I told you so' in their caring for you.

So your family may have inner conflicts of their own about your divorce, and it could be that you will get embroiled in that, and have less chance to attend to your own feelings.

## THE REACTIONS OF YOUR FRIENDS

Close friends can react in a similarly fault-placing manner. This is particularly true if you and your ex-wife knew them equally well. They may feel that they cannot remain friendly to both of you. Perhaps they will feel that they don't want to take sides, so they'll keep a distance from both of you so as not to offend either one of you.

Above all, be prepared to find that other couples may feel threatened by your divorce. Couples tend to socialize with other couples, and a divorce in one couple can make other couples feel self-conscious about their own problems. I was told by one man that after separating from his wife he went to stay with a friendly couple they had known for years. Within weeks this couple was having quarrels about who caused the break-up; the husband tended to side with him, the wife with his ex-wife. Although this was an undercurrent, and they did not row in front of him, this atmosphere made the environment uncomfortable and forced him to leave his friends' house.

Of course, family and friends can be a great source of comfort and help. However, there are pitfalls when it comes to living with them after your marriage has broken up.

Be prepared to find that this may be a period when

friendships change. It isn't just couples who take sides or become distant. You may find that someone you believed to be a good friend turns out not to be able to cope with the times when you are depressed. Several of my interviewees spoke of how they resented the friends who always kept trying to cheer them up. As one of them said: 'I got the definite impression that he didn't so much want to cheer me up, as shut me up.'

It will almost certainly be a time when you find that you make new friends. In this period, it may well turn out that women make better, more tolerable friends than men. To quote the same interviewee:

> 'I think it's fair to say that when I was married and, you know, just working in the day, going home at night . . . I never saw women as just friends. But since I've been divorced I found the reliable friends are women; and I don't mean girl-friends, I mean real friends . . . generous people, often.'

Relatives and friends can provide the help and comfort you may need, but it is also likely that you will want some sort of sexual relationship when you and your wife part.

## TRANSITIONAL SEXUAL RELATIONSHIPS

Why 'transitional'? I use this word because a man newly separated is going to go through a period of rapid change. As he changes, so his needs will change.

When the realization of his loss hits him, a man will need a relationship that will steady him and support him in a turbulent period. A sexual relationship at that point in his life will be important because good sex has a healing quality. A man who had recently just left his wife said:

164

'My new girl-friend is very good for me, very good. Sexually it's a relief to be with someone and feel, "This makes me feel so healthy!" I feel alive for the first time in years.'

This life-enhancing experience is very important in this, indeed *any*, phase of life. There were other men who described their new relationships as a 'comfort':

'She makes no demands. It's very nice having no demands made on you. I'm free to do what I want, when I want.'

This is the kind of relationship where the couple are likely to outgrow each other. The relationship works for each of them at the moment; however, I did wonder whether it would last if she asked my interviewee for a bit more commitment.

I have called those relationships 'transitional' because they can help you through a difficult, painful phase. There is nothing wrong with this, and it is often possible that the sexual aspect of the relationship fades and the lover becomes a friend. What *is* important, though, is to recognize that the relationship is transitional and so may not be permanent. If both partners are honest and considerate about this, then there is no reason why transitional relationships should not be, in their own way, a uniquely positive experience for both the man and the woman. It is important to avoid a situation like this:

'If I'm honest, I knew it wouldn't last. But I didn't want to say it, you know, straight out. I thought I'd lose her straight away. So I kept shtum. And then, for God's sake, she only gets pregnant.'

As a result, she had an abortion and he lost her anyhow. The woman concerned was in her mid-thirties, and very much wanted children. However, she did not want to bring them up on her own. It upset her so much to abort the child that their relationship could not stand the strain.

Often the most unstable transitional relationships are those that are clearly 'rebound' affairs. One of my interviewees told me that his marriage had been a disaster because he had previously been in love with a girl who rejected him. He was so devastated by this that he married her best friend 'on a rebound'. The best friend was a complete character opposite. The girl he loved was vivacious, the friend was placid.

> 'I had enough excitement, I just wanted peace, so I could say to myself, "Well, as regards women, that's that."'

Not surprisingly, this marriage did not last more than a few years, and his wife left him for a man who felt she was more than just a safe port in a storm.

Transitional relationships that are based on the new girlfriend being a complete character opposite to the ex-wife are likely to be short-lived. It is understandable for a man to want to experience the relief of, say, a placid, gentle woman when his wife has been demanding and aggressive. However, the wife's character must have answered some of his needs and her character-opposite may, eventually, begin to frustrate him.

Transitional relationships are often unbalanced, because one partner is more emotionally needy than the other. The arrangement will work only whilst it suits one person to give more than they receive. However, it is possible that a transitional relationship can transform into something more permanent. For this to happen, the giving and receiving will have to become more equal. It may turn out that a crisis over this sort of issue will reveal to the partners whether or not their relationship has a long-term future.

## MOVING IN WITH A LOVER: A NEW BEGINNING?

If you have had an affair whilst married then it may seem that the logical consequence of moving out of your home is to move in with your girl-friend.

This will create all sorts of tensions. Your ex-wife may well be distinctly more hostile towards you. The reasons for this are obvious: her sense of being rejected will be much keener if she feels that when she is alone in bed, you are enjoying the pleasures of love with your mistress. It will be much more difficult to make access arrangements because she will be reluctant to let the children visit you. The presence of your girl-friend will make her feel she is being supplanted as a mother, as well as a wife. Having said that all this is obvious, I think it is worth mentioning that one of my interviewees was perplexed and cross that his ex-wife did not want to meet his new girl-friend.

Other longer-term problems may arise. The relationship between a husband and his lover is, to some extent, unreal. Firstly, it is triangular: the ex-wife is the lovers' ever-present co-partner in any affair. It is difficult to make the transition from this situation to one where the two lovers are now living as if they were man and wife. In chapter three we saw how Lawrence and his girl-friend still needed his wife as an *éminence grise* to reassure them that they were Good, Sexy and Normal; she was Bad, Inhibited and Twisted. The perpetuation of that triangular relationship was keeping everyone stuck in an unreal world. Lawrence was keeping himself in a somewhat juvenile frame of mind by this division of the women in his life into goodies and baddies.

Extra-marital love affairs are, to some extent, secret. This is the second aspect of their *un*reality. The lovers can only meet at certain times in certain places, and the time they have together often feels special. That feeling can well disappear when they move in together. They may find that their time together is now not special, but ordinary. In short, the lovers may now be disappointed in each other and their relationship, discovering aspects of each other's character that were previously hidden.

This is all an inevitable part of the way *any* relationship develops. However, former lovers have other pressures on them. They have to deal with a certain amount of guilt at the destruction of the man's marriage. The man may begin to think, 'Was she worth it?' when he feels bad about deserting his ex-wife and children, if he has any.

Furthermore, the money situation will almost certainly be tight. The man is likely to be paying for two households from a wage intended for one. His girl-friend may find that she is, in part, supporting him.

All these factors may place abnormal pressures on a relationship that is, in many ways, new. The former lovers are getting to know each other for the first time as a couple. The man may also be trying to understand and come to terms with the fact that he loved, married but betrayed another woman. He may easily find it is not a haven where he can simply be himself, and allow himself to go through all the contradictory emotions that betrayal engenders. In fact, the situation can be so pressured that it traps the ex-wife, ex-husband and rival in mutually hostile attitudes. Trapped like this, it is very difficult for anyone to make a new start because the divorced couple are still stuck in their old lives.

It is certain that a divorced man will need to have the sort of comfort that family, friends and lovers can bring. However, all these people will have views and needs of their own which may, at times, infringe on his independent thoughts and so create fresh problems. It is important to realize this and to see that the need for this sort of comfort does not necessarily mean that you have to live with the comforter.

## LIVING ALONE

It is equally certain that a divorced man will need time to be alone. In chapter five, we saw that being alone is not the same as being lonely. It can be a great relief and, indeed, pleasurable, simply to have time to yourself. That said, the obvious drawback to living alone is that you can't have someone's company on demand; you have to arrange to see people.

The worst aspect of living alone is that, at times, you can feel that somehow you have been left alone to deal with life's problems, and that no one is on your side. It can make you feel so isolated that you begin to feel you are losing the ability to make contact with others. These feelings are not necessarily the result of having your own room, flat or house. They are aspects of the depression which follows the break-up of a marriage. Living with someone else will not heal that depression; company can provide a distraction, a temporary relief, but the basic problem remains, and only time will heal it.

The best aspect of living alone is that it can help you feel your life belongs to you. This is the result of taking charge of decisions about time and living space.

This is valuable if you have come from a marriage that felt restrictive. Living as a couple structures your time and the space you live in; you may discover that structure was, in fact, alien to you.

'After I had my own place a few months, I realized that I felt this tremendous relief at not having the whole living-room filled with ornaments, pictures, photos, and stuff. That's how my wife liked it, and it had to be. As you can see, I like the space free and uncluttered. Once I was living like this, the way I wanted, I really began to feel OK. It was amazing such a little thing had a big effect on me.'

This man was a designer; the layout of his house was important to him. This was part of a more profound realization:

'As time has gone on, I've come to realize that in the ways that really matter to me, my wife and I were totally incompatible. We have different politics, and totally different tastes. I wonder how we ever got round to being married at all. We've become more different as time has gone on.'

The most important realization was this:

'The great thing is that, now it's in the open – the fact we're such opposites – I like her much more. We're friends now. She's remarried, and she's fine. I'm happy about that. We were never suited really.'

The reason why he can be more relaxed about his wife is because he feels his home and his life are his own now. Therefore he can let his ex-wife have her home and life the way she wants it.

'I like living alone. Before, I was afraid to be alone; now I can enjoy the pleasure of doing nothing if I feel like it.'

This final comment shows that losing the fear of being alone can be part of the healing process that takes place when the mourning is allowed to run its course. Living alone need not be a kind of exile. It can be a way of exercising choice so that you see the people you want to see, when you want to see them. This can lead to a greater appreciation of what family, friends and lovers can offer. It can give you space and time in which to sort out what you really do need from your different relationships.

Aloneness is, after all, a basic fact of human existence, and it has to be faced sooner or later. The best expression of this is a short poem by the Sicilian poet, Salvatore Quasimodo:

> Everyone is alone on the heart of the earth
> pierced by a ray of sun;
> and suddenly it's evening.

Discovery of your real strengths, your real weaknesses, of what you really want in relationships, what you want out of life; all this can come out of the period after your marriage has ended. The rest of this chapter is about some ways of thinking out these issues.

## HIDDEN ASSUMPTIONS

In this book, I have tried to bring out some of the assumptions that we make about such issues as maleness, feelings, sexual attraction, being a couple, loneliness, parenthood, money and assets.

This technique of trying to find out what people *assume* is something you can do for yourself. It is merely a process of going back two stages. Look behind what someone says to what they are thinking. Then look behind what they are thinking, and try to see what assumptions underly those thoughts. This can be very useful when it comes to dealing with legal issues. As we've seen, those in the legal system are working on an adversarial principle, so they assume that divorce cases are a matter of winning or losing. Similarly, judges and others assume that fathers are less important as parents than mothers.

Knowing this can give you a great deal of power. Even in a situation when it seems that 'experts' have all the information and superior skills, you can challenge something you feel is wrong. The best basis for this is to bring into the open what you think they are assuming. You can politely say to a solicitor something like: 'Do you think a divorce can be won in the same way as a criminal case? Is one of us right, and the other wrong?'

You can say respectfully to a judge or a social worker something like: 'Do you think that for children a father is a less important parent than its mother?'

The effect of this is to bring the hidden issues into the light. Information will be seen in a different way because you have changed the context in which it is interpreted. It is possible then to discuss the basis on which choices and decisions are made. The discussion is not then based on a hidden agenda that everyone is following but no one will admit exists.

Above all, this technique is useful applied to yourself. You can begin to understand your own feelings, thought-processes and moods much better if you try to search out your own assumptions. This may help you to see a pattern in your choices and behaviour. Discovering your own hidden assumptions can reveal a previously hidden pattern in your life.

## HIDDEN PATTERNS

The end of a marriage is a natural time in which to think about why you married your wife and why it went wrong. This at least gives you a chance to avoid similar mistakes in the future. It is likely that you will see ways in which your marriage fitted in with the pattern of previous relationships, going back as far as your life with your parents.

We all, usually, choose to marry someone who is in the idiom of our mother or father. It isn't as simple as a man marrying someone just like his mother and this being something sick. It is normal to choose a partner whom you love and who will love you in a way you have learnt about love. Where do we first learn about love? From our parents, of course.

Problems can arise in adult sexual relationships if you follow an unhealthy pattern set down in childhood. This is now an accepted fact, but it is not easy to know what to look for when trying to seek out this pattern.

It is helpful to look first at the strongest negative emotions you have and ask: Is there a similarity between what you felt as an adult, and what you felt as a child? In all this, your own emotions will guide you: we store up and can remember feelings from long, long ago.

From here on it is a detective story. You look for all the clues you can. Trivial or otherwise; everything is important. The best example of how this kind of thinking works came in an interview I had with a marriage counsellor:

> 'A middle-aged man came to me to seek help with his second marriage. It was going the same way as his first. We looked for similarities together.'

What follows is my summary of the twenty weeks of counselling sessions:

His two wives seemed to be quite opposite. However, the counselling work revealed that they resembled each other, and his mother, in apparently trivial ways.

First, they had all given up work in their mid-twenties. They did this in different ways: his mother stopped working to have children. His first wife changed careers and the second career did not work out, so the work aspect of her life fizzled out. His second wife experienced a sort of a psychological block about following a promising career.

Second, all three women chose to live in out-of-the-way places, unreachable without a car. His mother settled in the country. When he met his first wife she was living in a caravan in a field. His second wife chose to live in the middle of a suburban complex miles from a train station. She had no car.

The end result of these two factors was that he was compelled to make difficult journeys to see his mother and both of his wives when courting. When he did marry, he ended up supporting both wives financially and emotionally. The third similarity was that all three women had a very limited sense of humour, and took everything very seriously.

During the sessions, the client and his counsellor looked at the significance of these similarities. The pattern that emerged was that all three women were rather afraid of the world. You can tell this from the first two points which show how they retreated from the everyday turmoil of life. The third point shows that all three were basically quite depressed.

The breakthrough came when all these facts helped the client to realize that, all his life, he had felt that to love someone meant that you provided them with everything they needed in life. To love someone meant to service them. His emotional reward was that he would be the one person in the world who would make life liveable for the person he loved. He had learned this from his relationship with a mother who was very unhappy: he wanted to make her better.

It was not surprising that neither he nor the relationships could take the strain of such an unequal balance of give and take. Both broke up within five years.

## NEGATIVE CAPABILITY AND THE 'SELECTED FACT'

Counselling of this sort can, after a while, help the client reassess what he needs from an adult sexual relationship. However, before this man could find the way to have love without constantly needing to service someone, it was vital for him to recognize the hidden assumptions he was making about love itself.

There is a way of doing this for yourself. It is really a matter of *not* doing things. Allow your emotions to lead you, and take in and consider all the ideas, memories or events they evoke. Then live with them. Just allow yourself to feel and contain what may be contradictory emotions. You are simply allowing your unconscious mind to tell you things. Conscious striving after explanations only inhibits the unconscious.

What *can* happen is that a clue will appear by itself that will point you in the direction of a solution. The distinguished analyst W. R. Bion calls this 'the selected fact'. This vital clue arrives by itself without you striving, working or straining. All you have to do is exercise what Keats called 'negative capability'. He defined this as 'capable of being in uncertainties, mysteries, doubts, without irritable reaching after fact and reason'.

## PSYCHOLOGICAL TIME WARPS

When someone constantly repeats patterns in their life, then it can be a sign that something drastic has happened to prevent them developing beyond a particular phase in life. The client discussed above will learn, through life or counselling or both, that it is likely he needs a more equal relationship.

Life can deal terrible blows which can trap a person in a sort of psychological time warp. This point is well illustrated by the story of Jack. He was very anxious to tell me about his life and his three failed marriages. He wanted to talk because he felt there was indeed a pattern, but he could not understand it.

My first impression was of a youthful man, full of enthusiasm and energy. He was obviously highly intelligent. His was a forceful personality, but not unpleasantly so. He was attractive in a rather boyish way. He was forty-three, and had had several careers: as a salesman, an inventor, a catering manager and had, in the past, owned his own hotel. He had been successful in all these careers.

This is particularly impressive because Jack did not have a good start in life. His father died of cancer on Jack's fourteenth birthday. A year later, Jack's brother was killed in a car crash. Jack said of this traumatic period, 'I don't think I felt it at the time, but it obviously had an enormous effect later.' He summed it up as follows: 'From living in a happy family of four, I was suddenly a boy living alone with my grieving mother.' Despite these problems, by the age of nineteen Jack was a successful salesman and electronics expert, earning good money. At twenty-two he was voted 'salesman of the year' by the local chamber of commerce.

Yet his life as a whole was not a success story. He had no property or assets of his own, and no savings. All his three marriages ended in divorce and financial ruin.

In fact, all Jack's marriages followed exactly the same pattern. He met all three wives at the same point in his career.

PHASE ONE: The Meeting.

Jack is just beginning to establish himself in a new job. He is beginning to be successful, well thought of and is clearly a man on the way up. He then meets a girl. (He calls them all 'girls'. He describes none of his wives as 'women'.) He goes out with the girl for a few months and suddenly they get married. There is no period of living together, or just getting to know each other; he proposes marriage. The three wives all have one character trait in common: none of them seems to be a strong, supportive partner. Jack does not choose someone who will help and support him as he makes his way in life. He actually chooses someone who is the very reverse. He describes his first wife as obsessively tidy, constantly trying to cramp him, make him conform and also very emotionally tied to her parents. He describes his second wife as 'a rather lonely girl', and his third wife as 'depressive'. Certainly he chooses three girls who are all going to take more than they can give.

PHASE TWO: Drifting apart.

After a period of about a year which seems to be relatively happy, Jack and his new wife begin to 'drift apart', as he describes it. When I ask for details of this, what emerges is that at this point in each marriage, Jack gives all his attention exclusively to work. He works long hours, weekends, gets home late. Obviously all three wives feel he is neglecting them, and react accordingly. His first wife demands that Jack buys a new house next door to her parents. His second wife has an affair. His third wife invites her sister and the sister's boy-friend to live with them.

So, in all three marriages, Jack has chosen a person who finds it hard to be left on their own. Then he neglects them. As a consequence, his home life alters drastically. Wives one and three both react by bringing in another couple. Jack is now no longer part of a twosome, but part of a foursome. With wife two there is the same change from a couple to a foursome, but it happens in a different way: she becomes pregnant; as Jack is now running a hotel, and Christmas is busy, he sends wife two plus baby to stay with her parents. She meets another man and they have an affair.

Marriages one and three continue after this point, but marriage two ends. None the less, Jack has so arranged it that he goes from being intimate with one woman to being emotionally involved with three people.

Some comments now on Jack's attitude to marriage and work.

It would be easy to see Jack as rather selfish and uncaring, neglectful of his poor wives whom he sacrificed to his ambitious desire to succeed in business. Yet he did not seem to be as cold as this implies, nor as ruthless. In fact he was very anxious to provide his wives with everything they wanted in the way of material goods. He was generous to a fault, offering to help their relatives financially. Moreover, he was at pains to point out to me that he did, after his second marriage ended, realize that he himself was to blame for his wife having an affair, that he had been selfish, and that he had neglected her. He told her he was sorry. Then he married again and repeated the pattern.

Jack's attitude to work was imbued with emotion. He described himself as 'entrepreneurial'. He loved new ideas. He also greatly enjoyed succeeding where others had failed.

Work for him was exciting, ever-new, and gave him a thrill that made him feel he was truly alive. Throughout the interview, Jack described all his work projects with all the enthusiasm of a man in love. He never described any of his women with such passion. Describing his work, he recalled every name, place and incident with ease. When I questioned him about his marriages, his recall of incidents was sketchy and very generalized. When I asked him what kind of contact he had with people through his work, he singled out two sorts of relationship. First: running a hotel gave him a feeling of being head of a big family, and the same feeling was created by running any work team. Second: he loved rubbing shoulders with the rich and famous, and greatly admired them. He was particularly in awe of 'professionals', like Cliff Richard.

PHASE THREE: Consolation in work as home breaks up.
Phase three has Jack losing himself in his beloved work in order to avoid going back to a home that is no longer his. It has been taken over by the other couple.

In marriage one, the wife's parents, now living next door, begin to invade the marriage. They insist that they come on holiday with Jack and his wife, and that the two couples eat together on a regular basis. Jack feels that his wife's parents side with her to make him conform to a middle-class, suburban idea of marriage. He finds home stifling, and reacts by taking on even more work. This is happening in the early 1960s when a financial boom makes it easy for Jack's new ideas to get backing.

In marriage three, his wife's sister and her boy-friend turn up and demand to be given a home and to be kept. Jack does not turn them away; he lets them stay, and puts his own money into their doomed financial projects, such as a record made by his wife and sister. Whilst he is giving them money they are also stealing it from him. They simply swindle him. Still he does not get rid of them; he forgives them, and so they continue.

Throughout this phase Jack works harder than ever.

PHASE FOUR: Marriage ends, Jack leaves, bankrupt.
Marriages one and three both end with Jack rebelling and walking out.

Marriage one: his wife and parents are having Sunday lunch, and Jack is expected to be there. In fact, he is in a pub (he recalls its name and what he was drinking) with a man (he recalls his name, too) and both are concluding a lucrative deal to produce fibreglass boats. Jack returns, flushed with success, and is told off for being late for lunch. He is incensed and walks out. Wife and parents sue Jack and he is declared bankrupt.

Marriage three: Jack finds that his wife and the other couple have now run up enormous debts, and allowed his hotel to run down. He does not tell them to go, does not mount a financial salvage operation; he sells the hotel at a ridiculously low price, thus bankrupting himself. Only now is he free of his wife and the other couple.

In all three marriages, Jack ends up in the same position: with one suitcase, and about £5 in his pocket. He is quite proud of this: 'They used to say of me, here he comes, the man with a suitcase, here he comes again . . .' More seriously, he believes, 'When you've got absolutely nothing, no money, nothing, then you can begin again.' And he does exactly that. He starts again, a new career, with a new girl. He seems to welcome this: when marriage one ended in bankruptcy he gave away his last £5 to a beggar. When marriage three ended he left his suitcase on the platform long enough for it to be stolen. He seems to want to have nothing. Then he can start.

★

Is he happy with the way his life has gone? In a way, yes. But he now feels he has wasted so much time, life and money, and wants to stop. That is why he admitted he knew there was a pattern, but could not see what it was or why it happened.

The pattern, and its cause, are clear if you look at the numbers. Jack goes from marriage (two), to two couples (four), to leaving home (one).

Jack never went through that phase in adolescence where the child grows in independence, forms his own opinions, rebels, quarrels with his parents and makes it up, tests the world out and finally leaves home to start his own life, with his parents' approval. He could not do that because his family was decimated. 'From living in a happy family of four, I was suddenly a boy living alone with my grieving mother,' as he said. Jack never went through that phase in his adolescence, so he had to repeat it in his marriages. He did this by:

*Phase one:*   Choosing a woman similar to his own mother, in that she was more needy than he was.

*Phase two:*   Engineering a situation that turned the clock back, taking him from living alone with one woman to living in a family of four.

*Phase three:*   Behaving in such a way that this 'family' became intolerably oppressive to him. He could then rebel, quarrel and –

*Phase four:*   Finally leave, to start a new life.

If it were really that simple, he would have done this once, and then moved on. However, Jack seemed to be stuck, doomed to repeat the same behaviour and feel the same feelings. There was something in this conflict which he could not resolve.

Jack loved his father very much. He also loved his brother. Both died at the point where Jack would have begun this phase of rebellion and making his own life. Both these bereavements created problems for Jack.

How could he tell his much-loved but dead father that he did not need him any more, and that he wanted to make his own way in life? To have said that to a man 'who I saw waste away before my very eyes' would have made Jack feel enormously guilty.

Why should Jack be permitted to grow up healthy and have his own life, be happy and prosperous, when his brother was 'cut down by a drunk driver' on a road that 'we both would bike along every day, a favourite route'. His brother's death left Jack with the guilt of a survivor: he continually asked himself 'Why should I be alive, and not him?'

These are enormous emotional problems for anyone to face. Jack's solution to them made them much worse. As he said, he 'didn't feel it at the time'. He blanked it out, and scrubbed round the problem by channelling all his energies into manic activity which he called 'work'.

Many of my interviewees adopted this technique for avoiding emotional problems: they abused work.

Obviously it's commendable to love your work and be dedicated to your job. You are very lucky if you have work that is fulfilling. But, like other pleasures, work can be abused, and thus become a drug. Drug abuse leads to addiction. The purpose of any addiction is to live a life where all your emotions are stimulated by impersonal objects or activities. Doing this cuts you off from human contact.

This abuse of work – simply filling your mind with practical problems – is one way of driving out your pain. It is very common for recently divorced men to do this; if it is for a limited period, it is harmless. It becomes dangerous if it develops into a way of life.

If this happens, then the work addict is not just avoiding pain, but adopting a lifestyle which will eventually put him beyond the reach of the only power that can heal his pain: the concern and love of other people.

Addiction to work, like other forms of addiction, cannot solve the underlying emotional conflicts that cause this pain. Addiction only masks the problem.

Jack told me he had worked almost every day of his life, including weekends. When he ran a hotel his idea of relaxing was to rewire the whole building. When I asked him how he felt if he was unemployed or stopped working he said:

'I just get very depressed, and . . . (*he struggles to find a word*) . . . oh . . . very black. Black.'

That was probably just the very beginning of how he felt about these two deaths. Beyond that 'blackness' were the conflicts he still had to face between those dead men and himself.

Facing up to and accepting emotional pain is very, very hard. It is difficult to see that all the 'blackness' is actually a door into oneself. Beyond that door is an inner world in which positive feelings are entangled with negative feelings. Perhaps your loving, tender emotions are tangled up with painful feelings and anger at losing love. Perhaps your capacity for hope and optimism is entangled with bitter disappointment. This ambiguity is very common when love, or a loved one, dies. This is what is going on in that inner world.

It is not so surprising. We are always full of contradictory feelings, even when life is going well for us. Falling in love or having a great success can brew anxiety as easily as it fills us with joy. You may be in love, but you could lose that love. You may have succeeded, but can you repeat the success next time round?

All this is a fact of life. As we have seen all through this book, what matters is that we allow ourselves to live with these contradictions. If we do this, then we are allowing ourselves to digest our experience in the same way we digest food. Experience – painful or joyful – can give the mind and heart nourishment in the same way food nourishes the body.

Mourning is a return to health because when we digest our experience, we go through a process of sifting the positive from the negative. In this way, the mind and heart work just as the body does: it, too, separates what is nourishing from what is waste.

We create problems when we block this process. We starve ourselves of nourishment, and fill ourselves up with waste products. We need nourishment in order to grow. Jack's example illustrates well how blocking this process can stunt emotional growth.

Jack had never faced the conflict with his father, he was stuck permanently at the age of fourteen. This explains why at forty-three he was full of new ideas, but had no home of his own. It explains why he could not be passionate about women, why they were all 'girls'. It explains his awestruck attitude to the rich and famous and his feeling that he could never be one of them. It explains why he had had no relationship with his real son, but had 'played' at being head of a big family whilst running hotels. Sadly, he placed his moments of real happiness as being before his father's death, when he was thirteen. He described this in lyrical terms: 'We would sit in the green fields in the sun . . . everybody was happy.' Jack could not get beyond this point. This was made very clear when I asked him what had made him most happy since then. He told me of the time he met Barnes Wallace, inventor of the Bouncing Bomb. He, of course, was the same generation as Jack's father, and both shared enthusiasm for planes. Jack said of the meeting, 'We sat in the sun, on the grass, and just talked for hours . . . I was so happy.' There was no such happiness with his wives or son. After talking to Jack for two hours, I began to feel there was something a bit desperate in his constantly boyish vitality. Surely, at forty-three, one could expect a greater range of emotions? Avoiding that conflict kept him stuck at an adolescent stage of development.

I have dealt with Jack's life in detail because it brings together a number of the themes that run through this book. Like so many of the men I interviewed, Jack assumed that if he gave in to his feelings of grief and loss, then he would lose control of himself and his life. In fact the opposite is true: he refused to allow himself to mourn the loss of his father and brother, forcing these emotions underground. However, they emerged with a vengeance and took over his entire life, forcing him to act out the conflicts he should have resolved in his adolescence.

It is significant that no one had ever challenged Jack with the (to him) heretical question: 'Why do you need to spend so much time working? What are you avoiding through working every hour God gives?' This was because Jack, his wives and colleagues all accepted the assumption that men are made male through work; the more he works, the more manly the man. So Jack's true emotional problems all went unnoticed because society wholly endorsed his way of avoiding them.

Jack's case is extreme; that is why it is useful. It shows the lengths we can go to to deny and stifle our true feelings about loss. It shows how it is possible to get trapped in a cycle of deprivation. If you use, for example, work to avoid your feelings, it can become an addiction that cuts you off from what is truly healing – the love and care of others. Above all, Jack's case shows that if you block the process of mourning, then you can limit your life to such an extent that you cannot achieve your full potential in work or in love. Certainly life dealt Jack cruel blows. However, his way of dealing with them, endorsed by society's view of what makes a man male, damaged him as much as the initial loss.

It would be possible for Jack to begin to solve his problem at any moment. He is stuck in the teenage time warp only because he has not paid attention to the grieving young Jack he has within him. The moment he acknowledges that this side of him exists, that it has urgent needs, and it demands to be heard, then the process of healthy mourning can begin. In mourning we heal ourselves. It is a natural process, and its purpose is to restore our hope, optimism and energy. Healthy mourning can help us make a new start and a new life.

# Summary

## COPING, LEARNING, STARTING AFRESH

At the end of chapter one, I suggested that it was useful for a recently divorced man to see himself as someone who has been injured. Separation is the emotional equivalent of being knocked over by a car. Divorce is like a long, major illness.

I want to use this metaphor in my summary of the self-help ideas in this book. I wanted to write a book that would help divorced men to cope with and learn from their experiences. Here is how to begin:

### YOU'RE INJURED

The first thing to do is admit it.

### LOOK AFTER YOURSELF

Don't pulverize your body with overwork. Don't bludgeon your feelings into silence with drink or drugs or loveless sex. It is better to rest, eat well, keep healthy and try to have some fun. Since you are ill, let yourself be ill and be looked after; that way, you'll get better.

### LET YOURSELF FEEL WHAT YOU FEEL

Feelings are not dangerous to you if you just let them be, and let them run their course. Suppressed, unacknowledged feelings are like viruses; they infect you. Expressed, acknowledged feelings are like an inoculation; they pervade your whole system, and eventually trigger your immune defence; they don't infect, they protect.

## LISTEN TO YOUR FEELINGS

When you feel bad, there is a reason. Pain is information about the injury. If you ignore the pain, you throw away the chance to heal the injury and avoid being injured again. The pain of loss, for example, can tell you a lot about what is precious to you. If you feel good, don't take it for granted. The pleasure of someone being kind to you can tell you a lot about what you need from a relationship.

## LET OTHER PEOPLE IN

Losing security, love, and a sense of belonging means you need to establish contact with the world in a new way. It is easy to get shut in with only your injury and grievances for company; let other people know you are there, and how you feel. If they withdraw it is because the emotions stirred up by divorce are a threat to them. They fear that your strong feelings will infect them and their lives. This is *their* problem, not *yours*. If you are straight about how you feel, you'll find out who can take it, and who can't. Learn to value the people who are strong enough to withstand that fear of being infected.

## RESIST REVENGE AND PUNISHMENT

If you are in pain, it is easy and tempting to lash out at others in the hope that it'll make you feel better. It helps, for a moment or two, but it does not last. You are almost certainly going to feel this way about your ex-wife; you'll believe that punishment and revenge will purge your own pain. And it does, momentarily. But do not use your children to punish your ex-wife. If your wife is using them in this way, tell her what she's doing. Have your rows direct with each other; argue about the loss of love. Don't fashion weapons made of assets or your children's needs. If you do, everyone gets wounded, including you.

## TRY TO FORGIVE

Whatever happened in your marriage happened for a reason. Try to understand those reasons and the part you and your wife played in the breakdown of the marriage. If she hurt you, try to see why and then try to work your way towards forgiving her. If you hurt her, try to see why, and then try to work your way towards forgiving yourself. It isn't easy, but living with the truth of what happened will help. Above all, whatever happened then, it is important to see that you and your ex-wife now share an important experience. That experience has injured you both; and you both hurt. Use your knowledge of pain to understand her pain.

## LOOK OUT OF THE WINDOW

Illness and injury, hurt and pain shut you in, at least to start with. There is a world out there full of possibilities and new beginnings. You'll be ready for them sooner or later. Good luck.

# Contact List

Here is a list of organizations that can offer help and advice on different aspects of divorce.

*Advice for couples and individuals who are considering separation or divorce*

RELATE (formerly The National Marriage Guidance Council)

Herbert Gray College, Little Church Street, Rugby CV21 3AP (Tel: (0788) 73241/565675)

They have local branches throughout the country. Head office will advise you whom to contact.

INSTITUTE OF FAMILY THERAPY

43 New Cavendish Street, London W1 (Tel: (01) 935 1651)

FAMILY CRISIS COUNSELLING SERVICE

Bishop Creighton House, Lillie Road, London SW6 (Tel: (01) 385 8400)

SCOTTISH MARRIAGE GUIDANCE SERVICE

26 Frederick Street, Edinburgh EH2 2JR (Tel: (031) 225 5006)

*Advice for those who seek special help because of religious belief or ethnic origin*

WESTMINSTER PASTORAL FOUNDATION
23 Kensington Square, London W8 (Tel: (01) 937 6956)

JEWISH MARRIAGE EDUCATION COUNCIL
529b Finchley Road, London NW3 3LG (Tel: (01) 794 5222)

CATHOLIC MARRIAGE ADVISORY COUNCIL
15 Lansdowne Road, Holland Park, London W11 3AJ (Tel: (01) 727 0141/2)

ASIAN COMMUNITY ACTION GROUP
Advice and Counselling Centre, 322 Brixton Road, London SW9 (Tel: (01) 733 7494)

AFRO-CARIBBEAN COMMUNITY CENTRE
355 Grays Inn Road, London WC1 (Tel: (01) 837 1841)

If none of these groups is appropriate, it is worth asking for contact numbers at your local Citizen's Advice Bureau. Your local library will also have a list of support groups. These are usually kept in the Reference section.

*Advice for those having problems with the legal side of divorce*

Choosing a solicitor is a chancy business. If you decide to use your own solicitor who has handled your other legal needs, make sure that he or she has experience in handling *both* divorce *and* conveyancing.

If you want a second opinion, go to your local Citizens Advice Bureau. They will give you a list of local solicitors. For a reasonable fee you can set up a single consultation in which you can discuss your legal problems and receive advice which will help you decide whether your own solicitor is acting in your best interests.

Similar legal advice can be obtained from your local Law Centre.

CABs and Law Centres and the Solicitors Family Law Association will help you find a solicitor.

CITIZENS ADVICE BUREAU CENTRAL OFFICE
110 Drury Lane, London WC2B 5SW (Tel: (01) 836 9231)

SOLICITORS FAMILY LAW ASSOCIATION
c/o 154 Fleet Street, London EC4A 2HX (Tel: (01) 353 3290)

## *The conciliation service*

There is a network of conciliation services in this country. To obtain information and a list of conciliation services in your area, contact:

DIVORCE AND CONCILIATION ADVISORY SERVICE
38 Ebury Street, London SW1 0LU (Tel: (01) 730 2422)

Like most counselling services, this organization does not seek to reconcile an estranged husband and wife. They try to make the process of separation easier, and the legal aspects of divorce acceptable to both parties.

*Help and advice over problems with children, and for single parent families*

GINGERBREAD

35 Wellington Street, London WC2E 7BN (Tel: (01) 240 0953)

NATIONAL COUNCIL FOR ONE-PARENT FAMILIES

255 Kentish Town Road, London NW5 2LX (Tel: (01) 267 1361)

ORGANIZATION FOR PARENTS UNDER STRESS (OPUS)

26 Manor Drive, Pickering, N. Yorkshire YO18 8DD (Tel: (0751) 73235).

PARENTS ANONYMOUS

6–9 Manor Gardens, London N7 6LA (Tel: (01) 263 8918)

FAMILIES NEED FATHERS

Elfrida Hall, Campshill Road, London SE13 (Tel: (01) 852 7123)

PROBLEMS WITH STEPCHILDREN

9 Cottage Lane, Chasetown, Walsall WS7 8XZ

NATIONAL STEPFAMILY ASSOCIATION

Maris House, Maris Lane, Trumpington, Cambridge CB2 2LB (Tel: (0223) 841306).

## Problems created by homosexuality within marriage

SIGMA
Tel: (01) 837 7324

## For those seeking individual counselling and therapy

Your own GP will give you a letter of referral. However, you may not want to use a family doctor in this way. Furthermore, it may take time to find suitable counselling or therapy under the NHS.

If you feel you need therapy, you can contact the following organizations. Choosing a therapist is rather like choosing a good solicitor. It is not vital that you *like* the therapist; but you do have to feel that you can confide in this person. They must inspire trust in you; so shop around a bit.

TAVISTOCK CENTRE
120 Belsize Lane, London NW3 5BA (Tel: (01) 435 7111)

INSTITUTE OF PSYCHOANALYSIS
63 New Cavendish Street, London W1 (Tel: (01) 580 4952)

PSYCHOTHERAPY REGISTER
1 Wythburn Place, London W1 (Tel: (01) 724 9083)

THE PSYCHOTHERAPY CENTRE
67 Upper Berkeley Street, London W1 (Tel: (01) 723 6173)

CONTACT LIST

CENTRE FOR PSYCHOTHERAPY
8 Willow Road, London NW3 (Tel: (01) 794 8717)

It is easier to obtain this kind of help in London than in other parts of the country, but the numbers above should provide you with enough information to put together a list of therapists in your area.

There are also many weekend courses you can attend. Beware of those courses that charge an extortionate fee, claiming they will change your life. They are almost certainly bogus. A weekend course can, however, help you begin to understand yourself a little. And you'll meet others who share similar problems.